SMALL &
CONTAINER
GARDENING

SMALL & CONTAINER GARDENING

A practical guide to gardening in small spaces

PETER MCHOY & STEPHANIE DONALDSON

BARNES
&NOBLE
BOOKS
NEW YORK

This edition published by Barnes & Noble, Inc.
by arrangement with Anness Publishing Limited

2001 Barnes & Noble Books

M 10 9 8 7 6 5 4 3 2 1

ISBN 0 7607 2309 5

Publisher Joanna Lorenz
Managing Editor Judith Simons
Project Editor Mariano Kälfors
Designers Patrick McLeavy & Partners, Bill Mason, Janet James and Ian Sandom
Photographers John Freeman, Debbie Patterson,
Janine Hosegood and Marie O'Hara
Jacket Designer Nigel Partridge
Production Controllers Ben Worley and Joanna King

Printed and bound in Hong Kong

CONTENTS

Introduction   6

THE SMALL GARDEN   8

ELEMENTS OF DESIGN   12

Planning Your Garden   14

Difficult Sites   38

FEATURES AND STRUCTURES   56

The Garden Floor   58

Forming Boundaries   84

Finishing Touches   102

Rock and Water Gardens   126

CHOOSING PLANTS   140

Beds and Borders   142

Planning Borders   148

Maintaining Beds and Borders   180

Plants for a Purpose   188

The Kitchen Garden   220

THE CONTAINER GARDEN   230

GETTING STARTED   234

Decorating Containers   270

THE PLANTING PROJECTS   276

Colour Schemes for Containers   278

Seasonal Planters   328

Edible Collections   378

Scented Collections   394

Difficult Situations   408

Inspirational Containers   418

The Young Container Gardener   448

Indoor Containers   462

PLANT GUIDE   484

GARDENER'S RECORDS   486

INDEX   504

ACKNOWLEDGEMENTS   512

Introduction

Small gardens can be a blessing in that they do not require a lot of hard work to create and maintain. But this is no reason to settle for a patch of lawn and a few hardy plants. Your garden is very much a part of your home it pays to give it the kind of attention that you would the inside of your house.

The hard landscaping (paving, fences, paths, walls) gives the garden its design. Hedges or careful screening can hide a garden shed or the place where garden refuse is stored, and at the same time add interest to the garden. It is important to keep the design simple, as most of a small garden can be seen at a glance; however, it is an advantage if the garden does not show all its attractions at once. Individual features or focal points like benches, urns, birdbaths, lights or well-placed containers arranged singly or in groups, draw the eye and add an extra dimension to the garden.

Choice of the right plants can enhance the general landscaping, providing the flesh, shape and texture of the garden. The size of plants is also important in a small garden. Taller plants can be used for architectural effects and give the garden height, but plants that are too big can overpower a small garden. Tiny plants, planted in the cracks or paving stones or walls, add texture and colour.

Plants maintain the visual interest in the garden. By choosing the appropriate plants you can ensure that your garden is a picture all year round. Bulbs provide colour in spring with welcome signs that a new year is beginning. Berries and foliage attract the birds and turn into autumnal reds

and browns, evergreens keep the interest going in winter, annuals and perennials make up a kaleidoscope of colour, or enhance a colour-themed garden, throughout the year.

Containers also play their part in year-round visual interest. By planning their planting carefully, not only do they provide colour and interest in their own right, but by placing them in a flower bed after a plant has finished flowering or in a newly empty space, they can continue to delight the viewer. Apart from creating beautiful displays outside, planting in containers is also an easy and extremely versatile way to bring the garden inside.

Plants have other purposes too. They can be planted for shade or shelter, as screens for privacy, for

their scent, to attract butterflies and birds to the garden, and to harvest fruit and vegetables for the home, or herbs for the cook.

The small garden can be designed to be one that is easily maintained, an ongoing hobby or a challenge. It can also become a place to sit out on a summer's day, a play space for children or an outdoor room. Whether you are a novice or an experienced gardener and plantsman, this book will help you make the garden of your dreams a reality.

BELOW: *A garden can be many things, but ultimately it is a place of relaxation. A vibrant display of plants on the wall and potfulls of plant colour creates an instant and irresistable al fresco room.*

OPPOSITE: *Family gardens have to be multi-purpose. If you do lots of entertaining, then a barbecue and seating area is likely to be a priority. A bright or colourful tablecloth will transform a drab table in an instant. Add a few pots of seasonal plants for that finishing touch.*

The Small Garden

• Planning your Garden • Difficult Sites
• The Garden Floor • Forming Boundaries
• Finishing Touches • Rock and Water
Gardens • Beds and Borders • Planning
Borders • Maintaining Beds and Borders
• Plants for a Purpose • The Kitchen Garden

These are expensive gardens to create, slow to establish, and labour-intensive to maintain, but the results can be stunning. This kind of garden is unsuitable for a young family.

Formal herb gardens

Herb gardens are popular features and are much easier to create than knot gardens. Illustrations of both old and new herb gardens in books will often give you ideas for designs.

Rose gardens

A formal rose garden is easy to create, and it will look good even in its first season. To provide interest throughout the year, edge the beds with seasonal flowers and underplant the roses with spring bulbs or low-growing summer flowers.

Paved gardens

A small garden lends itself to being paved throughout. By growing most plants in raised beds or in containers, less bending is involved and many of the smaller plants are more easily appreciated. Climbers can be used to make the most of vertical space, and if you plant in open areas left in the paving, the garden can still look green.

Courtyard gardens

Space can be at a real premium in the heart of a town, but you can turn your backyard into an oasis-like courtyard garden, with floor tiles and white walls that reflect the light. Add some lush green foliage, an 'architectural' tree or large shrub, and the sound of running water. Although the plants may be few, the impact is strong.

Traditional designs

A small formal garden, with a rectangular lawn, straight herbaceous border, and rose and flower beds is still a popular choice with gardeners looking for the opportunity to grow a wide variety of plants such as summer bedding, herbaceous plants, and popular favourites such as roses. The design element is less important than the plants.

LEFT: *The use of white masonry paint can help to lighten a dark basement garden or one enclosed by high walls.*

BELOW: *This long, narrow plot has been broken up by strong lines: a useful design technique.*

Informal effects

The informality of the cottage garden and the 'wilderness' atmosphere of a wild garden are difficult to achieve in a small space, especially in a town. However, with fences well clothed with plants so that modern buildings do not intrude, an informal garden can work even here.

Cottage gardens

The cottage garden style is created partly by design and the use of suitable paving materials (bricks for paths instead of modern paving slabs), and also by the choice of plants.

Relatively little hard landscaping is necessary for a cottage garden – brick paths and perhaps stepping-stones through the beds may be enough. It is the juxtaposition of 'old-fashioned' plants and vegetables that creates the casual but colourful look associated with this type of garden.

Mix annuals with perennials – especially those that will self-seed such as calendulas and *Limnanthes douglasii*, which will grow everywhere and create a colourful chaos. If flowers self-sow at the edge of the path, or between other plants, leave most of them to grow where they have chosen to put down roots.

Plant some vegetables among the flowers, and perhaps grow decorative runner beans up canes at the back of the border.

Wildlife gardens

A small wildlife garden seems almost a contradiction in terms, but even a tiny plot can offer a refuge for all kinds of creatures if you design and plant with wildlife in mind.

Wildlife enthusiasts sometimes let their gardens 'go wild'. However, this is not necessary. A garden like this one looks well kept and pretty, yet it provides long vegetation where animals and insects can hide and find

RIGHT: *The house itself will inevitably dominate a small garden, especially when you look back towards it. Covering the walls with climbers will help it to blend in unobtrusively.*

food. There is water to attract aquatic life, and flowers and shrubs to bring the butterflies and seeds for the birds.

An orchard can also be a magnet for wildlife of many kinds.

Woodland gardens

A woodland effect is clearly impractical for a very tiny garden, but if you have a long, narrow back garden, trees and shrubs can be used very effectively. Choose quick-growing deciduous trees with a light canopy (birch trees, *Betula* species, are a good choice where there's space,

RIGHT: *The woodland effect can be delightfully refreshing on a warm spring or summer day, but works best with trees that have a tall canopy that allows plenty of light to filter through. Although a pond is attractive in this situation, care will have to be taken to remove leaves in the autumn.*
BELOW: *A pretty pond is a super way to attract wildlife, and looks especially good if well integrated into the garden like this one.*

but they can grow tall). Avoid evergreens, otherwise you will lose the benefit of the spring flowers and ferns that are so much a feature of the traditional woodland garden.

Use small-growing rhododendrons and azaleas to provide colour beneath the tree canopy, and fill in with ground cover plants, naturalized bulbs such as wood anemones and bluebells, and plant woodland plants such as ferns and primroses.

Use the woodland effect to block out an unattractive view or overlooking houses. As an added bonus it is low-maintenance too.

Rocks and streams

Rock or water features alone seldom work as a 'design'. They are usually most effective planned as part of a larger scheme. Combined, however, rocks and water can be used as the central theme of a design that attempts to create a natural style in an informal garden.

Meandering meadows

Instead of the rectangular lawn usually associated with small gardens, try broadening the borders with gentle sweeps, meandering to merge with an unobstructed boundary if there is an attractive view beyond. If the distant view is unappealing, take the border round so that the lawn curves to extend beyond the point of view. Use shrubs and lower-growing border plants to create the kind of border that you might find at the edge of a strip of woodland.

Bright beds and borders

If plants are more important than the elements of design, use plenty of sweeping beds and borders, and concentrate heavily on shrubs and herbaceous plants to give the garden shape. Allow plants to tumble over edges and let them grow informally among paving.

If you want to create a strong sense of design within such a plant-oriented small garden, use focal points such as ornaments, garden seats or birdbaths.

Distant influences

Professional garden designers are frequently influenced by classic styles from other countries, especially Japan, but amateurs are often nervous of trying such designs themselves. Provided you start with the clear premise that what pleases you is the only real criterion of whether something works, creating a particular 'foreign' style can be great fun. Adapt the chosen style to suit climate, landscape and the availability of suitable plants and materials.

Japanese gardens

'Real' Japanese gardens are for the purist who is prepared to give the subject much study. Raked sand and grouped stones have special meaning for those briefed in the Japanese traditions, but can be enigmatic to untrained Western eyes.

Many elements from the Japanese style can be adapted for Western tastes, however, and many gardeners are happy to introduce the essential visual elements without concern for deeper meanings. This style is easily adapted to a small space, and the uncluttered appearance makes a confined area appear larger.

Stone and gravel gardens

Although stones and rocks are widely used in Japanese gardens, they can also be key components in creating a garden which is more reminiscent of a dry river bed in an arid region – the sort of garden that you might find in a rocky, semi-desert area.

This kind of garden needs minimal maintenance, and if you choose drought-tolerant plants it should look good even in a very dry summer.

Stone gardens appeal to those with a strong sense of design, and an adventurous spirit, rather than to plant-lovers. Although the plants play a vital role in the drama of the scene, opportunities for using a wide range of plants is limited.

Gravel gardens are also a practical choice where space is limited. You can add some large boulders or rocks as focal points, and plants can be used much more freely. It is easy to plant through the gravel, and a wide range of plants can be grown in groups or as isolated specimens.

LEFT: *You don't need a lot of plants to create a Japanese-style garden. Strong hard landscaping and the restrained use of plants is a hallmark of the Japanese garden style.*

OPPOSITE TOP: *The use of formal water, painted wall and patio overhead gives this garden a Mediterranean atmosphere.*

OPPOSITE: *The dry gravel slope and the use of plants like yuccas help to create the illusion of a garden in a warm, dry climate.*

Mediterranean gardens

The illusion of a Mediterranean garden is most easily achieved in a backyard or tiny walled garden. The effect is difficult to achieve if you view neighbouring homes and gardens over a low fence – guaranteed to kill any self-deception as to location!

Paint the walls white, or a pale colour, to reflect the light and create a bright, airy feeling. If possible include alcoves in which you can place plants, or build ledges on which you can stand pots.

Pave the area with bricks, terracotta-coloured pavers or tiles – but steer clear of paving slabs. Use plenty of decorative terracotta pots and tubs.

The illusion is completed by using plenty of appropriate plants, such as pelargoniums, oleanders, bougainvilleas, and daturas (brugmansias). Stand pots of large cacti and succulents outdoors too.

The success of this kind of garden owes less to its structural design than to the use of appropriate plants, ornaments, and garden furniture.

Exotic effects

You can give your garden an exotic appearance by concentrating on exotic-looking plants that are hardier than

their appearance might suggest. Grow them in pots on the patio (which will enable you to move the tender kinds to a greenhouse or conservatory, or just a sheltered position, if you garden in a cold area), or in a gravel garden.

Tough, spiky plants to consider for this kind of garden are many of the hardy yuccas, and phormiums if they grow in your area without protection. Add some agaves such as *A. americana* if you live in a very mild area.

Palms are associated with warm climates, but some are tough enough to withstand moderately severe winters. *Trachycarpus fortunei* is particularly reliable. Just a few well-chosen plants can create images of far-away places.

Getting the details right

One of the most difficult tasks when planning a small garden is working out how best to use the available space. For most of us, it is the decorative features – the plants themselves – that take priority. But functional features are important, too, and it is best to allocate space for these first.

Once the fundamentals have been dealt with, it is much easier to decide where you want to have planting areas. Within this framework, you will be able to transform the space into a decorative outdoor room that you will want to use for much more of the year than just the few summer months.

Practical considerations

You will probably have decided that you want somewhere to sit. This need not necessarily be next to the house. For example, if evening is the time of day when you will most often be able to sit outside, and there's a spot at the far end of your garden that catches the evening sun, then it makes sense to site your seating area here.

If you have children, you will probably want somewhere for them to play. Common sense dictates that this is near the house, to make supervision easier. Try, if you can, to include a sandpit – children will be thrilled with one just 1m (3ft) square; if there is just a little more space, there will be room enough for a small play house.

Although there is a temptation to banish such mundane essentials as the tool shed and the compost bins to the bottom of the garden, with a long site this will not be very practical. Consider giving them a more central position, suitably screened from view all round.

Plan out in your mind the best place for each of these features in much the same way as you might plan your kitchen, where you also need to make the best possible use of the available space to make it efficient to work in and comfortable to be in.

RIGHT: *By dividing up the spaces, you can create visual depth. These two spectacular box orbs help to define a vista and lend perspective to the arbour at the end.*

Making changes

Once these priorities are fixed, it will be much easier to work out the layout of the garden. This is important, even if you don't have the resources for new paving and landscaping, at least for the foreseeable future. For example, there may be a flower bed just where you feel it would be best to create a seating area. With the garden layout left as it is, you would continually

ABOVE: *This wall hides part of the garden, offering privacy, while the archway frames a statue, bringing perspective to the whole space.*

BELOW: *Secret places can be created in even the smallest of spaces. This pathway winds through plantings in a tiny 3m (10ft) plot.*

ABOVE: *Even the smallest of spaces may be transformed with decorative touches such as pots of colourful primulas in a wooden holder.*

have to bring furniture in and out when you need it. That is no more comfortable than a living room would be if you had to bring in a chair every time you wanted to sit down. However, with a few little changes, like simply turfing over the flower bed, you can organize the garden so it is ready for relaxation any time you want.

Planning for privacy

Privacy and shelter are essential requirements for relaxation in the garden but, especially in built-up areas, they can be difficult to achieve. Try fixing trellis on top of walls and fences to create extra height. You can then grow decorative climbers to provide a wonderful natural wallpaper. You could plant fast-growing conifers such as thuja, although you should always check their potential final height or you could end up deeply overshadowed, if not overlooked.

Seating areas in particular need privacy. Even if you live in the middle of the country, you will feel much more comfortable if you site these where, at least on one side, there is the protection of a wall of some sort. This could be the garden boundary wall, a hedge, or even a trellis screen to lend a more intimate feel.

Overhead screens

If you are closely overlooked, you may also want to create privacy from above. One of the most successful ways of doing this is to put up a pergola and let it become entwined with vines or other climbers. That way, you have a 'roof', which filters the natural light and allows a free flow of fresh air.

Creating the right atmosphere

Creating the right mood for your garden depends on stimulating the senses: sight, sound, touch, taste and smell, all of which are supplied free of charge by nature. And simply by being outside, you are closer to nature, so it should be even easier to bring atmosphere to the garden than to anywhere else in your home. For many people, the garden is just as important as any room in the house.

Sight and sound
You will find a wealth of suggestions for stimulating the senses throughout the following pages. These ideas can be set against the visual delights provided by the plants themselves. As well as the sound of birdsong and buzzing insects, you can add the music of wind chimes or the evocative trickling of water in even the smallest plot.

Smells galore
The outdoors also provides the most glorious fragrances, both sweet – from flowers such as roses, honeysuckle, and jasmine – and aromatic – from lavender and piquant herbs. Remember that scent develops in the warmth of the sun, so choose a sunny spot and that after a spring or summer shower, the air can smell heavenly.

Touch and taste
Touch, too, can be stimulated as it is impossible to walk through a garden without being touched by – or reaching out to touch – some of the plants. This is especially pleasing if they have interesting textures. Plan for a variety of these, using plants with fleshy, frondy and feathery leaves. Finally, eating out in the garden completes the sensory picture.

ABOVE: *A pretty Victorian-style wire plant stand, filled with flowering plants, brings flashes of bright white high up in the middle of a largely green planting area.*

LEFT: *The sound of trickling water enhances any outdoor area, and a water feature need not take up a large amount of space. Water flows over this wall-mounted, cast-iron shell.*

ABOVE: *A courtyard is set out as an outdoor room, with a cherry tree suggesting pretty 'wallpaper' and blossom forming a carpet.*

ABOVE: *Brick-shaped paviours set into a tiny lawn, then decorated with urns mimic the vistas set out on the floors of classical gardens.*

A hint of romance

The most romantic gardens hint at intimacy. They could literally be enclosed outdoor rooms, such as courtyards, balconies or roof gardens, which automatically offer intimacy. If your space is rather larger, you can add romantic interest by creating hidden places. This isn't difficult, even in the smallest garden. You can put a door in the fence or wall to hint at another space beyond; put up an archway to give the feeling of moving from one area to another; or add a trellis screen to section off an eating area or enclose a garden seat.

Creating an illusion

As well as creating intimacy, these dividing tactics also give the illusion of space. Adding an archway or screen means you are able to see beyond into another area, which lends perspective to the whole space, giving it structure and shape. However light the resulting screening is, it hints at secret places and romance.

LEFT: *A series of basic motifs painted over stripes of vibrant colours gives simple pots a rich Mexican look.*

Focal points

Focal points are an essential part of good garden design, relevant whatever the size of garden. They help to take the eye to a favourable part and away from the less favourable. They can also act as signposts to lead the eye around the garden and placed at the end of the garden they can lead the eye into the distance, thus making the garden seem larger than it is in reality.

Adding interest to lawns

An expanse of even a well-kept lawn may look bare and a little boring, especially if all the interest is in the beds and borders around the edges. It can be useful to create a focal point within the lawn, but this often works best if offset to one side or towards one end of the lawn, rather than in the centre. Position it where you want to take the eye to an attractive view, or use it to fill an area that lacks interest. Try to avoid placing the focal point against a background that is already busy or colourful; otherwise one will fight against the other for attention.

Birdbaths and sundials

A sundial is a popular choice for a focal point on the lawn, but should be placed in a sunny position if it is to look in the least credible. A birdbath is another favourite option, and is especially delightful if it is close to the house where the visiting birds can be seen and enjoyed.

Statues and plants

In a small garden, a spectacular focal point such as a statue can be used to dominate a corner of the garden so that the limitations of scale and size become irrelevant for the moment. Bear in mind that plants can be used as well as inanimate objects. While a well-placed ornament or figure will serve as a simple focal point, when used in conjunction with plants, the effect can be particularly striking.

LEFT: *An exquisite, weathered wood and metal door makes a decorative garden entrance while the statue draws the eye towards the doorway.*

RIGHT: *A formal geometric pond with its oriental overtones makes a charming focal point in a terraced town garden.*

FAR RIGHT: *An enchanting little pond, complete with fountain and cherub, mimics designs on a much grander scale.*

Gateways and arches

Gateways and arches make excellent focal points in a garden, and can add a feeling of mystery and promise from whichever side you view them. Both gateways and arches work best if the areas on either side of them are laid out in contrasting styles or are visually very different to each other. In a long, narrow garden, for example, you could produce a series of arches or gates, taking the eye further on into a journey of exploration.

ABOVE: *A tripod can be used to draw the eye to the end of the garden. Once fully grown this Clematis 'Jackmanii' will cover it completely.*

RIGHT: *Beneath this metal walkway, Greek pithoi in a bed of euphorbia and hellebores are used to great effect as a focal point.*

Screens and disguises

Unless you are extremely fortunate, there will be a certain view or some objects within the garden that you really want to hide. Focal points can be used to take the eye away from some of them, but others will require some form of screening or disguise. A little bit of trickery can even be used to make the garden look a different shape – to shorten the appearance of a long thin site, for example, or to give apparent depth to a garden that is wide but shallow.

Living screens

Many common hedging plants can be allowed to grow taller than normal to form a shrubby screen. Space the plants further apart than for a hedge, so that they retain a shrubby shape, and clip or prune only when it is necessary to keep within bounds. Avoid a formal clipped shape unless you are screening within a very formal garden. Most hedging plants will grow to twice their normal hedge height if you give them more space and do not restrict them by frequent clipping and pruning.

Matching screen and setting

Choose plants appropriate to the setting. In a Japanese-style garden, many of the tall bamboos will make an excellent screen for, say, a garage wall or oil storage tank. Use shrubby plants in a garden where there are lots of shrubs, and especially if the shrub border can be taken up to the screening point. On a patio, a climber-covered trellis may look good.

Urban solutions

In town gardens, and particularly in the case of balcony and roof gardens, the problem is to minimize the impact of surrounding homes, offices and factories. These usually require impracticably huge walls to mask the view, which would also make the garden excessively dark. In a very small garden, trees may not be a practical solution for this type of screening either, although in a larger one they will probably provide the answer.

ABOVE: *Dense planting at the end of the garden suggests that the property goes further, even if the path leads nowhere in particular.*

A sensible compromise is to extend the wall or fence with a trellis, or similar framework, along which you can grow climbers. This will not block out the view completely, but it will soften the harsh impact of buildings and help to concentrate the eye within the garden by minimizing the distractions beyond. The boundary itself will be given extra height and interest.

Boundaries and beyond

A combination of plants and hard landscaping is often the most satisfactory way to screen a view beyond a boundary. Trees are a particularly pleasing solution. Even if they lose their leaves in winter, the network of branches is often sufficient to break up the harsh outline of buildings and beyond, and in summer – when you spend more

time in the garden and require more privacy – the canopy of foliage will usually block out most of the view. Trees are a particularly good solution if the aspect is such that most of the shadow falls away from your garden rather than over it.

Optical illusions

Although there are limits to how much you can change the site of your garden physically, it is possible to employ some optical tricks with which to alter its appearance.

A long, straight view will be foreshortened by a tall object or bright colours at the far end of it. If, on the other hand, the distant end has a scaled-down ornament and misty, pale colours, the ornament will appear to be further away.

Using colour and mirrors

A straight lawn can be narrowed towards the further end to make it seem longer, and the effect can be enhanced by using a bright splash of colour near the beginning. If your garden is wide but not very deep, you can give an impression of enhanced depth by positioning a mirror almost opposite the entrance and surrounding it with plants. As you step outside, you seem to see an entrance to another, hidden part of the garden.

If the area is surrounded by walls, they can be painted white (for extra light), green (to blend in), or with a floral mural where the planting is sparse. Shaped trellises can be added to give the impression of a distant perspective rather than a flat wall, and a false doorway with a *trompe l'oeil* vista disappearing away behind it can be wonderfully effective at enlarging a confined space.

OPPOSITE: *Here, painted square trellis has been used as a screen, dividing off one part of the garden from another.*

RIGHT: *A floral arbour makes a rich decorative frame for a piece of statuary, creating a very theatrical effect and hiding an unsightly view.*

ABOVE: *A cleverly positioned mirror will reflect the plants back into the garden, suggesting that it is larger than it actually is.*

ABOVE: *An ordinary, wooden-slat garden door leads from an alleyway to a tiny but enchanting city garden.*

Utilities and storage

The need to find room for less attractive bits and pieces of the garden – such as the dustbins (garbage cans) and the compost heap – is a fact of life, but utilities like these need not be on show. With a little imagination, they can be completely disguised or made to blend in with their surroundings. Storage space will also be needed for the amount of practical paraphernalia that gardening brings, from tools and pots and planters to potting compost (soil mix), seeds and string.

In an ideal world, dustbins (garbage cans) and recycling containers would be beautiful in themselves, but, unfortunately, in reality they are seldom an attractive sight. They are necessary, however, and they do need to be accessible. You can ignore your dustbins (garbage cans) or spend a little time and effort blending them in, by painting them to co-ordinate with the overall scheme (if this is feasible), using a screen of plants to hide them, or camouflaging them with a plant-covered trellis.

RIGHT: *A wire shelving unit, intertwined with clematis, makes a delightful garden detail that also serves a practical purpose.*

BELOW: *Shelving can be used for purely decorative purposes outside as well as in, no matter how small the garden.*

Compost bins

Compost is an invaluable aid for any gardener, no matter how small or large the plot. Material for composting can simply be piled in a heap in a corner and left to rot, but a manufactured container certainly looks more appealing. Various kinds of compost containers are available from garden centres. Those made of plastic tend to resemble rubbish bins (garbage cans), so why not treat them in the same way, either decorating them or screening them with plants. An alternative is to make your own container from suitably treated timber, painted to match the house or the rest of the garden furniture. The design can be very simple, with timber slats fixed to corner posts, or more imaginative – such as a compost bin in the shape of a traditional beehive!

Garden sheds

Garden sheds are the classic means of storing tools and equipment. Most gardens can accommodate one, although smaller gardens may be restricted to a mini-shed or tool store (cabinet), which can be as small as 30cm (12in) deep and so can be tucked into a corner. The shed need not be an eyesore: if painted and decorated it can become an attractive part of the garden architecture. Alternatively, you can camouflage the shed with plants climbing up a trellis. Fix the trellis to timber battens using catches rather than screws, so you will be able to remove both climbers and trellis when the shed needs another coat of preservative.

All-weather shelves

Another solution is to put your goods on show. Garden pots can be very attractive and, displayed on all-weather shelves, can become part of the decorative appeal of the garden. This is an excellent solution for very small gardens and patios, all of which still need space for practical elements.

Instead of buying ready-made garden shelving, you could build

RIGHT: *Every available space should be utilized in a small garden. Here, a box on a shelf has been used to grow a few vegetables.*

BELOW RIGHT: *These well-filled borders help to draw the attention away from a storage shed hidden in the corner of the garden.*

BELOW: *French baker's shelves against a house wall make a garden nursery for growing seedlings on – and do not take up much room.*

your own from timber and treat it with exterior-quality paint. Old metal shelves can be given a new life using car spray paint or specially manufactured metal paint, which can even be sprayed straight over rust.

All shelves should be fixed firmly to the garden wall – avoid fixing to the house wall as this could lead to damp (moisture) problems. Once fitted, use shelves for displays, to store tools, or for bringing on young seedlings, which can look delightful potted up in ranks of terracotta.

Basic patterns

Having decided on the *style* of garden that you want, and the *features* that you need to incorporate, it is time to tackle the much more difficult task of applying them to your own garden. The chances are that your garden will be the wrong size or shape, or the situation or outlook is inappropriate to the style of garden that you have admired. The way round this impasse is to keep in mind a style without attempting to recreate it closely.

If you can't visualize the whole of your back or front garden as, say, a stone or Japanese garden, it may be possible to include the feature as an element within a more general design.

STARTING POINTS

If you analyse successful garden designs, most fall into one of the three basic patterns described below, though clever planting and variations on the themes almost always result in individual designs.

Circular theme

Circular themes are very effective at disguising the predictable shape of a rectangular garden. Circular lawns, circular patios, and circular beds are all options, and you only need to overlap and interlock a few circles to create a stylish garden. Plants fill the gaps between the curved areas and the straight edges.

Using a compass, try various combinations of circles to see whether you can create an attractive pattern. Be prepared to vary the radii and to overlap the circles if necessary.

Diagonal theme

This device creates a sense of space by taking the eye along and across the garden. Start by drawing grid lines at 45 degrees to the house or main fence. Then draw in the design, using the grid as a guide.

Rectangular theme

Most people design using a rectangular theme – even though they may not make a conscious effort to do so. The device is effective if you want to create a formal look, or wish to divide a long, narrow garden up into smaller sections.

Circular theme

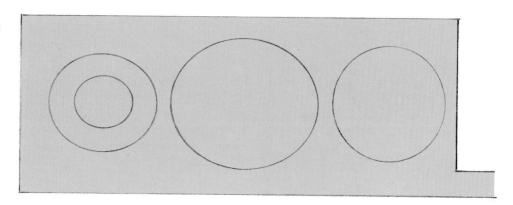

Diagonal theme

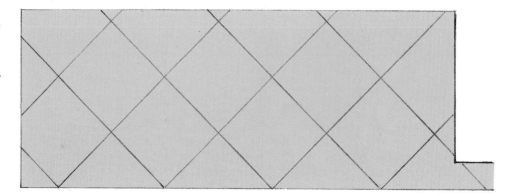

Rectangular theme

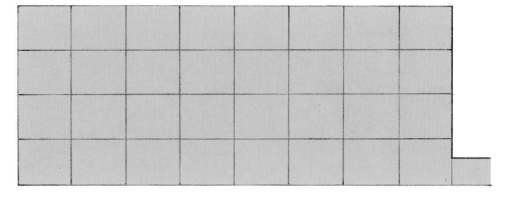

alleys and passageways between houses demand thoughtful planning and appropriate plants.

Front gardens present a special problem, not because of size or shape, but because a large portion of the garden is usually dedicated to the car – often there is a broad drive to the garage or a hard standing area where the vehicle is left for long periods. Legal restrictions about what you can do with your front garden can be another potential problem – especially on estates where the developers or local authority want to maintain an 'open plan' style.

If conditions really are too inhospitable for permanent plants, or the space too limited for a 'proper' garden, containers can provide the answer. Use them creatively, and be prepared to replant or rotate frequently so that they always look good, whatever the time of year.

Unpromising backyards and basements can be transformed as much by a coat of masonry paint, a few choice plants, and some elegant garden furniture and tubs, as by an extensive – and expensive – redesign. Imagination and inspiration are the keynotes for this type of garden design.

In this chapter you will find many solutions to specific problems like these, and even if your particular difficulty is not covered exactly, you should be able to find useful ideas to adapt.

ABOVE: *This long, narrow plot has been broken up into sections, with an angled path so that you don't walk along the garden in a straight line.*

LEFT: *Roof gardens are always cramped, but by keeping most of the pots around the edge it is possible to create a sense of space in the centre.*

Unusual shapes

Turn a problem shape to your advantage by using its unusual outline to create a garden that stands out from others in your street. What was once a difficult area to fill will soon become the object of other gardeners' envy because of its originality.

Long and narrow – based on a circular theme

This plan shows a design based on a circular theme. The paved area near the house can be used as a patio, and the one at the far end for drying the washing, largely out of sight from the house. Alternatively, if the end of the garden receives more sun, change the roles of the patios.

Taking the connecting path across the garden at an angle, and using small trees or large shrubs to prevent the eye going straight along the sides, creates the impression of a garden to be explored.

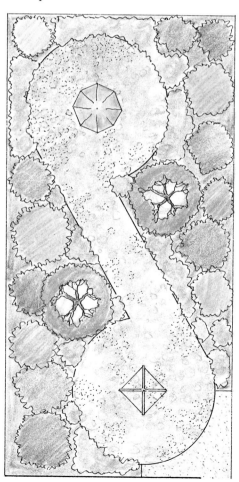

Long and narrow – based on diagonal lines

This garden uses diagonals to divide the garden into sections, but the objective is the same as the circular design. It avoids a straight path from one end of the garden to the other, and brings beds towards the centre to produce a series of mini-gardens.

Long and tapered to a point

If the garden is long as well as pointed, consider screening off the main area, leaving a gateway or arch to create the impression of more beyond while not revealing the actual shape. In this plan the narrowing area has been used as an orchard, but it could be a vegetable garden.

Staggering the three paved areas, with small changes of level too, adds interest and prevents the garden looking too long and boring. At the same time, a long view has been retained to give the impression of size.

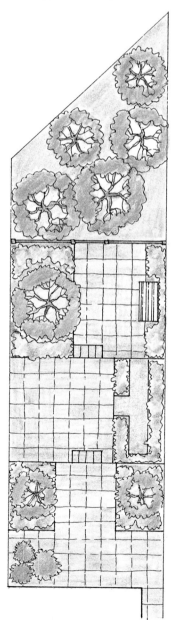

The shape of the roof will largely determine your design. Usually raised beds are built around the edge, with a sitting area in the centre. Pots can be used to provide variety within the paved area.

The roof is one place where artificial grass does have a place in the garden. Paving is heavy, artificial grass light. And it adds a touch of much-needed colour.

Keeping weight down

Do everything possible to keep down the weight. Avoid thick, heavy paving stones – if you do use paving, choose the thinnest. Use lightweight, loam-free potting composts (soil mixes), and plastic or glass-fibre containers rather than terracotta or wood.

Watering

Plants in containers need frequent watering in warm or windy weather. Carrying water to the rooftop is unappealing, and getting out a hosepipe (garden hose) to connect to a tap indoors is also cumbersome. Give some thought to installing an automatic watering system.

Using windbreak screens

A windbreak of some kind is likely to be an essential feature of a roof garden, since gusting wind and turbulence can play havoc with plants – and people. A windbreak screen can also be invaluable in providing privacy and in masking many of the unattractive features that a rooftop presents.

A structure that is partly permeable to the wind is much more effective than a solid one, where localized turbulence is created as the wind hits it and is deflected. Black windbreak netting becomes almost invisible if it is strung between two posts and then hidden behind a painted trellis, especially if plants are then grown up the trellis.

This form of windbreak is both effective and does not take up much room – an important consideration when space is at a premium.

ABOVE: *A roof garden can be quite spectacular, especially if the building is strong enough to take structural features such as those shown here.*

RIGHT: *Trellises provide privacy and shelter from the wind and can be fairly light which avoids increasing the weight.*

Using plants for protection

Where more room is available, a screen of tall, wind-tolerant shrubs installed along the most vulnerable side will act to shelter the area behind them. Many plants will tolerate this kind of exposure, while still providing colour and interest throughout the year. For a permanent screen, it is important to use mainly evergreen plants, although some of the tough deciduous shrubs can be included to add variety.

With this barrier in place, the effect of the wind should be considerably reduced, allowing you to complete a decorative planting scheme. As far as the space will

allow, plan for a staggered effect, using tall plants or small shrubs at the back, next to the windbreak screen, and moving through to ever smaller perennials and annuals. At the front, you should end up with a relatively warm, sheltered space, which is ideal for less resilient plants – delicate spring bulbs, for example.

Balconies and verandas

For someone without a garden, a balcony may be their entire 'outdoor room', a 'garden' to enjoy from indoors when the weather is inclement. Even more than a patio, the balcony or veranda is an outdoor extension of the home.

The area is usually small, so the money you are prepared to spend on gardening will go a long way. Splash out on quality flooring and furniture, and ornate containers, which will create a classy setting for your plants.

Choosing flooring

The floor will help to set the tone and style, and it can make or mar a tiny 'garden' like this.

Paving slabs are best avoided: they are heavy, frequently lack the kind of refinement that you can achieve with tiles, and the size of individual slabs may be too large to look 'in scale' for the small area being covered.

Think of the veranda or balcony floor as you might the kitchen or conservatory floor – and use materials that you might use indoors. Quarry tiles and decorative ceramic tiles work well, and produce a good visual link with the house. Make sure ceramic tiles are frostproof however. Tiles are relatively light in weight, and their small size is in proportion to the area.

Timber decking is another good choice for a veranda.

The problem of aspect

Aspect is an important consideration. Unlike a normal garden, or even a roof garden, the light may be strong and intense all day, or there may be constant shade, depending on position. Balconies above may also cast shade.

If the aspect is sunny, some shade from above can be helpful. Consider installing an adjustable awning that you can pull down to provide shade for a hot spot. Choose sun-loving plants adapted to dry conditions for this situation – your indoor cacti and

RIGHT: *Roof gardens and balconies are often improved if you lay a wooden floor and create a timber overhead.*

succulents will be happy to go outside for the summer.

If the aspect is shady for most of the day a lot of flowering plants won't thrive. You may have to concentrate on foliage plants, though some bright flowers, such as impatiens and nicotiana, do well in shade.

Countering the wind

Like roof gardens, balconies are often exposed to cold and damaging winds. The higher a balcony the greater problem wind is likely to be.

To grow tender and exotic plants, provide a screen that will filter the wind without causing turbulent eddies. A trellis clothed with a tough evergreen such as an ivy is useful, or use screens of woven bamboo or reeds on the windiest side – these not only provide useful shelter and privacy, but make an attractive backdrop for plants in containers.

Adding colour round the year

Create a framework of tough evergreens to clothe the balcony or veranda throughout the year, and provide a backdrop for the more colourful seasonal flowers.

Use plenty of bright seasonal flowers in windowboxes or troughs along the edge, with trailers that cascade down over the edge.

In the more sheltered positions, grow lots of exotic-looking plants, and don't be afraid to give lots of your tough-leaved houseplants a summer holiday outside.

Pots of spring-flowering bulbs extend the season of bright flowers, but choose compact varieties – tall daffodils, for example, will almost certainly be bent forward as wind bounces back off the walls.

Add splashes of colour with cut flowers. In summer choose long-lasting 'exotics' such as strelitzias and anthuriums.

ABOVE: *In mild areas or a sheltered position, you can turn your balcony into a tropical garden.*

RIGHT: *Turn your balcony into an outdoor room where many indoor plants thrive in summer.*

Features and Structures

Overall garden design is important, but it is individual
features that make a garden special. Major structural
decisions, such as the type of paving to use, the shape of the
lawn, or how to define the boundaries, have a significant
impact, but even small details like ornaments and garden
lights can lift a small garden above the ordinary. The use of
containers is especially important in a small garden – on a
tiny balcony they may *be* the garden. Use them imaginatively,
choosing containers that are decorative, and grouping them
for added interest.

ABOVE: *Create the urge to explore
with small paths that lead to features
such as seats and ornaments.*

OPPOSITE: *The garden floor is
important, whether paving or a lawn,
but it is features, like this arbour
and its seat, that give the garden
character.*

The Garden Floor

THE GARDEN FLOOR – LAWN, PAVING, PATHS, even areas of gravel or ground cover plants – can make or mar your garden. These surfaces are likely to account for more area than the beds and borders. Although they recede in importance when the garden is in full bloom, for much of the year they probably hold centre stage.

Removing existing paths and paved areas presents a practical problem. If they are laid on a thick bed of concrete you will probably have to hire equipment to break up the surface. Provided these areas do not compromise your design too much, it is much easier to leave as many as you can in position. Consider paving over the top with a more sympathetic material. It should be relatively easy to extend the area if you want to.

Lawns are more easily modified than paths and paved areas. At worst you can dig them up and resow or relay them. If you simply want to change the shape, you can trim off surplus grass or lift and relay just part of the lawn.

ABOVE: *Paths can be both functional and attractive, often giving the garden shape and form.*

OPPOSITE: *Hard landscaping, such as bricks, combined with soft landscaping, such as lawns, can look very harmonious if designed with integration in mind.*

OPPOSITE ABOVE: *A brick edging marks the boundary between lawn and border, and serves the practical purpose of making mowing easier.*

LEFT: *Areas like this would soon become weedy if not densely planted. Here hostas suppress the weeds, and Soleirolia soleirolii spills over onto the path.*

LAYING A LAWN FROM TURF (SOD)

Turf (sod) provides the best method of creating a lawn quickly – you can use it within a few months – and soil preparation is a little less demanding. You will usually find that it is a more expensive option than growing a lawn from seed, but many gardeners are happy to pay a premium for the convenience.

1 You should dig and consolidate the soil as described for seed, but there is no need to wait a few weeks to allow weeds to emerge – the turf (sod) will prevent weed seeds germinating. Start by laying the turf (sod) along a straight edge.

2 Use a plank to stand on while you lay the next row, as this will help to distribute your weight. Stagger the joints from row to row, to create a bond as if you were laying bricks. If using a long roll of turf (sod), there will be fewer joints. Make sure that these do not align.

3 Tamp down each row of turf (sod) (you can use the head of a rake as shown), then roll the plank forwards to lay the next row.

4 Brush sieved sandy soil, or a mixture of peat and sand, into the joints. This will help to bind the turves (pieces of sods) together

5 Shape edges when the lawn is laid. Lay a hose or rope to form the shape for a curved edge, or use a straight-edged piece of wood for a straight edge, and trim with a half-moon edger.

Weed-free paths and lawns

A weed-filled lawn will spoil your garden, but with modern weedkillers it is quite easy to eliminate weeds to leave your grass looking like a lawn rather than a mown wildflower meadow. It's easy, too, to clear garden paths of unsightly weeds – and to keep them that way.

Killing weeds in lawns and paths
The only place where weeds are really acceptable is in a specially designated wildlife corner, although some people find daisies and other so-called weeds in the lawn a very attractive feature. Generally, however, weeds have to be controlled, and pulling them up by hand is a time-consuming job that few of us enjoy. It is even more frustrating if they grow back again within a few days.

The method on the opposite page shows how easily you can deal with weeds in the lawn. Paths can also be kept weed-free for a season using one of the products sold for the purpose. Most of these contain a cocktail of chemicals which act

quickly to kill existing weeds and others that prevent the growth of new ones for many months. A single application should be enough to keep the path clear of weeds for a long time. It is a good idea to use an improvised shield to prevent the weedkiller being blown by the wind onto the flowerbeds while you are applying it to the paths.

ABOVE: *This garden illustrates the beauty of a well-maintained lawn that is free of weeds. The lawn in this garden is the perfect spot for a bird house, which will attract many local birds, and possibly squirrels, all year round. The addition of a couple of rose bushes adds elegance and interest to this very pretty garden.*

LEFT: *The most beautiful and expensive of paths can be marred by weeds. Either make sure they are mortared between the joints, or use a path weedkiller to keep them smart.*

KILLING WEEDS IN LAWNS

This method ensures a weed-free lawn with as little as one application a year.

1 Weeds in lawns are best controlled by a selective hormone weed-killer, ideally in mid- or late spring. These are usually applied as a liquid, using a dribble bar attached to a watering-can. To ensure even application, you should mark out the lawn with string lines, spacing them the width of the dribble bar apart.

2 Always mix and apply the weedkiller as recommended on the packet by the manufacturer. There are a number of different plant hormones used, some killing certain weeds better than others, so always check that the product is recommended for the weeds you most want to control. When mixed, simply walk along each strip slowly enough for the droplets from the dribble bar to cover the area evenly.

3 If your lawn also needs feeding, you can save time by using a combined weed and feed. The most efficient way to apply these products – which are likely to be granular rather than liquid – is with a fertilizer spreader.

4 If you only have a few trouble-some weeds in a small area, it is a waste of time and money treating the whole lawn. For this job a spot weeder that you dab or wipe onto the offending weed should work very well.

WORDS OF WARNING

Weedkillers are extremely useful aids, but they can be disastrous if you use the wrong ones, or are careless in their application.

- Always check to see whether it is a total or selective weedkiller.
- If selective, make sure it will kill your problem weeds – and make sure it is suitable for applying to the area you have in mind. Lawn weedkillers should be used only on lawns.
- Don't apply liquid weed-killers on a windy day.
- For greater control, use a dribble bar rather than an ordinary rose on watering-cans.
- Keep a watering-can specially for applying weed-killers, otherwise residues may harm your plants.
- Avoid run-off into flowerbeds, and if necessary use a shield while applying a weedkiller.

Caring for lawns in autumn

Autumn is a good time to prepare your lawn for the year ahead, and the best time to tackle any long-term improvements. Tasks such as raking out lawn debris as well as feeding and aerating will improve the quality of your lawn greatly if they are carried out every year.

1 Over the years, grass clippings and debris form a 'thatch' on the surface of your lawn. This affects growth of the grass and should be removed with a lawn rake.

2 If grass growth is poor, the soil beneath may have become compacted, preventing oxygen reaching the plant roots. You can aerate the lawn by pushing the prongs of a garden fork about 15cm (6in) into the ground.

3 Brush a soil improver into the holes made by the fork. Use sand or a mixture of fine soil and sand if the ground is poorly drained. Alternatively, use peat or a peat-substitute, or very fine, well-rotted garden compost if the ground is sandy.

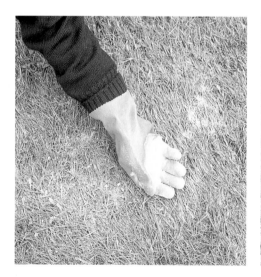

4 If your lawn is in poor condition and needs reviving, apply an autumn lawn feed. It is essential that you use one formulated for autumn use, as spring and summer feeds will contain too much nitrogen.

5 You can tidy an uneven lawn edge at any time, but doing it in autumn will mean one less job to do at busier times of year. Use a half-moon edger against a board held in position with your feet. This is not an annual job.

MECHANICAL AIDS

Working on large areas such as lawns can be exhausting and back-breaking work. Raking out thatch is a particularly tiring job. If you have a fairly large lawn area, it is definitely worth investing in a powered lawn rake. This will remove the thatch both rapidly and efficiently for you.

You can also take the sheer drudgery out of aerating your lawn by using a hollow-tined aerator that removes a core of soil effortlessly and efficiently.

If you need to remove a large quantity of leaves from your lawn in the autumn, you also might prefer to invest in a special leaf sweeper or blower.

Collecting and composting leaves

Never waste the leaves that accumulate in your garden. They will make excellent garden compost if you collect them and allow them to rot down.

In addition, if they are left on the ground, they can damage areas of grass as well as smother other small plants on the edges of beds and borders.

1 Don't let leaves lie for long on your lawn. The grass beneath them will turn yellow and be prone to disease. On a small lawn, rake them up with a lawn rake.

2 The leaves that build up on paths and drives are best brushed up with a broom or besom.

DON'T LET LEAVES SMOTHER SMALL PLANTS

If you let leaves lie for long on small plants such as alpines, they may begin to rot due to the lack of light and free movement of air. The leaves will also provide a haven for slugs and other pests that may eat your plants. Wait until most of the leaves have fallen from the trees, then go around and pick them off vulnerable plants.

3 You can buy special tools to lift the leaves without too much bending, but using two pieces of wood is also an effective method of lifting them once they have been brushed into a heap.

4 Leaves can be added to the compost heap, but some leaves rot down slowly, so it is best to compost large quantities on their own. Rotted leaves are also a useful addition to potting composts (soil mixes).

Naturalizing bulbs

Many spring- and autumn-flowering bulbs look delightful naturalized in a lawn. Planted at random among the grass and left undisturbed, they soon form large colonies, and will flower year after year. One possible drawback is that you won't be able to cut the lawn for several weeks after flowering, until the leaves have died down – although some people may see this as an advantage.

What to plant?

If you are lucky enough to have space in your garden to naturalize bulbs in lawn or an area of longer grass, then choose those bulbs that will multiply and flower freely. These include an array of spring-flowering bulbs such as crocuses, daffodils (*Narcissus*), snowdrops (*Galanthus*), small fritillaries (*Fritillaria*) and winter aconites (*Eranthis hyemalis*). Even planting just a few early-flowering tulips can create a spectacular swathe of bright colour. Although tulips look spectacular growing within the lawn, avoid planting them too close together because their broad leaves can smother the grass beneath.

Naturalizing is also an ideal way of growing colchicums: these are leafless at flowering time in autumn (the leaves appear later in the spring) and the grass will help to disguise the bare stems. Despite this these delightful plants are well worth growing for their large goblet-shaped, usually pink or white, flowers.

You can use a number of different bulbs, or grow just one type, and choose flowers all of the same colour, or an eye-catching mixture. Even if you decide to limit yourself to the familiar daffodils and crocuses, there are many different kinds of these bulbs to choose from, so you will have plenty of choice.

A variety of methods

There are several different ways of naturalizing bulbs. You can dig individual planting holes in the grass (satisfactory for just a few bulbs), or lift strips of turf (sod) to expose a larger area of soil for planting. Alternatively, if you have a lot of bulbs to plant over a wide area, then individual planting holes may be more appropriate than creating larger excavations to take a group of bulbs.

For more delicate bulbs, which won't be able to compete with strong-growing turf (sod), the best method is to plant them in bare but well-cultivated ground and sow a fine grass seed over the top.

HOW TO NATURALIZE SMALL BULBS IN GRASS

1 If you have a lot of small bulbs, such as crocuses and winter aconites, to plant in a limited area, it is best to lift sections of turf (sod) and plant the bulbs underneath. Use a spade to slice beneath the grass, then roll it back for planting.

2 Loosen the soil with a fork first as it will be very compacted, and work in a slow-acting fertilizer such as bonemeal.

3 Scatter the bulbs randomly. Very small ones can be left on the surface; larger ones are best buried slightly. Cover the bulbs with twice their own depth of soil. Roll back the grass, firm it well, and water.

DIVIDING ESTABLISHED CLUMPS

WHICH WAY UP

It is of great importance to check that a bulb is the right way up when planted, with the growing point upwards. Most bulbs have a very obvious top and bottom and present no problem. Others, especially corms and tubers, can cause confusion because they lack an obvious growing point. If you are in any doubt, it is best to plant them on their side – the shoot will grow upwards and the roots down.

A few bulbs that do have an obvious top are planted on their side because the base tends to rot in wet soil – although these are rare exceptions. *Fritillaria imperialis* is sometimes planted this way, and it is always worth planting vulnerable bulbs on a bed of grit or coarse sand to encourage good drainage around the base.

1 Naturalized bulbs and those left in borders for years will eventually need dividing to stop overcrowding, which will lead to deteriorating results. Lift very large clumps when the leaves have just died back, or any time when the bulbs are dormant.

2 Separate the clump into smaller pieces and then replant. You do not have to separate the clump into individual bulbs.

HOW TO NATURALIZE LARGE BULBS IN GRASS

1 Large bulbs such as daffodils are easier to plant using a bulb planter, which takes out a core of soil. Scatter the bulbs randomly over the surface so that the display will look natural.

2 Push the bulb planter into the soil, twisting it a little if the ground is hard, then pull it out with the core of soil. Place the bulb at the bottom of the hole.

3 Crumble some soil from the bottom of the core. Drop some of this into the hole to fall around the bulb and make sure it is not suspended in a pocket of air. Then press the core back into position.

Grass substitutes

Grass is still the best form of living carpet for a large lawn subject to wear, but small areas are ideal for experimenting with those alternatives to grass that will give your garden a highly individual touch.

None of the plants described will form such a hard-wearing lawn as grass, but they have their own attractions. Bear in mind that you can't use a normal selective lawn weedkiller on these broad-leaved plants, so be prepared for some hand weeding. On a small-scale, however, this is manageable, and a price worth paying if you fancy a lawn with a difference.

RIGHT: *For an attractive-looking lawn in a small area not subject to heavy wear, chamomile is ideal.*

BELOW: *Thyme is tough enough to grow between paving, where it is often crushed underfoot.*

Scent with chamomile

This classic grass substitute has been used for centuries to make an attractive, pale green lawn. The fact that it is aromatic when walked on combined with an ability to tolerate a reasonable amount of wear, makes it an excellent choice for a small, ornamental area. But, like the other plants suggested here, chamomile is not a practical proposition for a children's play area.

What it looks like Chamomile has small, feathery, aromatic leaves and white daisy flowers, though the non-flowering 'Treneague' is preferable as flowers spoil the close carpeted effect. It spreads rapidly by creeping stems, which is one reason that it makes such a good substitute for grass.

How to sow or plant You can sow seed, but the best lawns are established from young offshoots or cuttings of a non-flowering variety. If you buy seed, start them off in seed trays to produce young plants to put out later. If you buy young plants or offshoots by post they will probably arrive in a plastic bag – larger specimens from a garden centre will

be pot-grown but you will pay more.

Plant 23cm (9in) apart – closer if you have a lot of seed-raised plants or cuttings of your own. Close spacing will achieve quicker cover, but the final result is unlikely to be any better. If you are growing from seed, start off under glass in early spring, and plant out in late spring, rather than sow directly in the open ground like grass.

Trim with the mower set high to encourage the development of sideshoots if the plants do not seem to be making enough bushy side growth. You will have to mow flowering forms occasionally to keep the plants compact.

You may find chamomile under

one of its two widely used Latin names *Chamaemelum nobile* or *Anthemis nobilis*.

Thyme

Thyme is another popular alternative to grass for a small area, but be sure to choose the right kind of thyme. The culinary species is too tall and bushy for this purpose. Choose the more prostrate *Thymus serpyllum*.

Thymes are good for dry soils, and do well in alkaline (chalky) areas. Unfortunately they tend to become woody and straggly after about four or five years. Cuttings are easy to root, however, so periodic replanting should not be an expensive task.

What it looks like Thymes have small, aromatic leaves, and *T. serpyllum* has low, spreading growth 5cm (2in) high. Clusters of tiny purple, white, pink, red, or lavender flowers appear in summer.

How to sow or plant Plant about 23cm (9in) apart. You can raise your own plants from seed (sow in trays, not directly into the soil).

HOW TO PLANT A THYME LAWN

1 Prepare the ground thoroughly by digging over the area and levelling it at least a month before planting. Dig out any weeds that appear. Hoe off seedlings. Rake level.

2 Water the plants in their pots, then set them out about 20cm (8in) apart, in staggered rows (a little closer for quicker cover, a little further apart for economy but slower cover).

3 Knock the plant from its pot and carefully tease out a few of the roots if they are running tightly around the edge of the pot.

5 Water the ground thoroughly and keep well watered for the first season.

4 Plant at their original depth, and firm the soil around the roots before planting the next one.

ABOVE: *Clover – in this case wild white – makes a novel lawn, as gardeners usually spend so much time trying to eliminate it.*

Clover

If clovers seem to thrive better than the grass in your existing lawn, eliminate the grass and try a clover lawn – it will probably look greener than grass in dry weather! You will, of course, still have to weed, to remove non-clover seedlings.

What it looks like The three-lobed leaves of the clover are well known. The white or purple flowers should not be a feature of a clover lawn – mow the plants before they are tall enough to flower.

How to sow or plant Clover is sown in-situ, on ground cleared of weeds, ideally in spring. You can sometimes buy clover seed from companies specializing in wild flower seeds. White clover (*Trifolium repens*) is a good one to sow for a lawn.

Cotula

There are several low-growing species of cotula that can be used for a lawn. In some countries they are regarded as lawn weeds, in others lawns are sometimes created for them. They are worth a try if you are prepared for a rampant plant that may need curtailing.

What it looks like Cotulas are low-growing plants, with divided, fern-like leaves. The creeping stems root as they grow. Masses of small yellow flowers are produced in mid summer.

How to sow or plant Plant about 10–15cm (4–6in) apart. *Cotula coronopifolia* is the one usually used as a grass substitute. The cheapest way is to sow seed, but this is only likely to be available from suppliers dealing in the less common plants.

Imaginative paving

Most small gardens have a patio or at least a paved area close to the house. Often it is the main feature around which the remainder of the back garden is arranged. It can be the link that integrates home and garden. At its worst, paving can be boring and off-putting; at its best it can make a real contribution to the overall impact of the garden.

On the following pages you will find a selection of popular paving materials, with suggestions for use, and their advantanges and dis-advantages. Always shop around because the availability and price of natural stones vary enormously, not only from country to country, but also from area to area.

Even the availability of man-made paving will vary from one area to another. Choosing the material is only part of the secret of successful paving – how you use it, alone or combined with other materials, is what can make an area of paving mundane or something special.

LEFT: *Bricks and pavers often look more attractive if laid to a pattern such as this herringbone style.*

Colour combinations

Your liking for bright and brash colour combinations will depend on the effect you want to create. Be wary of bright colours though – they can detract from the plants, although they will mellow with age.

Sizing up the problem

In a small garden, large-sized paving units can destroy the sense of scale. Try small-sized paving slabs (which are also easier to handle), or go for bricks, pavers, or cobbles.

Mix and match

Mixing different paving materials can work well, even in a small space. Try areas or rows of bricks or clay pavers with paving slabs, railway sleepers with bricks, in fact any combination that looks good together and blends with the setting. Avoid using more than three different materials, however, as this can look too fussy in a small garden.

Paving patterns

You can go for a completely random pattern – crazy-paving is a perfect example – but most paving is laid to a pre-planned pattern using rectangular paving slabs or bricks. Look at the brochures for paving slabs. These usually suggest a variety of ways in which the slabs can be laid.

Although a large area laid with slabs of the same size can look boring, avoid too many different sizes, or complex patterns in a small space. Simplicity is often more effective.

Bricks and clay pavers are often the best choice for a small area, because their small size is more likely to be in harmony with the scale of the garden. The way they are laid makes a significant visual difference, however, so choose carefully.

The stretcher bond is usually most effective for a small area, and for paths. The herringbone pattern is suitable for both large and small areas, but the basket weave needs a reasonably large expanse for the pattern to be appreciated.

Stretcher bond

Herringbone

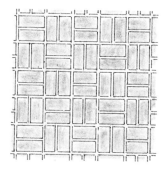

Basket weave

HOW TO LAY PAVING

1 Excavate the area to a depth that will allow for about 5cm (2in) of compacted hardcore topped with about 3–5cm (1–2in) of ballast, plus the thickness of the paving and mortar. As an alternative to hardcore topped with ballast, you can use 5cm (2in) of scalpings. Check the depth of the foundation before laying the paving. If adjoining the house, make sure that the paving will end up below the damp-proof course.

2 Put five blobs of mortar where the slab is to be placed – one at each corner, and the other in the middle.

3 Alternatively, cover the area where the paving is to be laid with mortar, then level.

4 Position the slab carefully, bedding it on the mortar.

5 Use a spirit-level to ensure that the slab is level, but use a small wedge of wood under one end to create a slight slope over a large area of paving so that rainwater runs off freely. Tap the slab down further, or raise it by lifting and packing in a little more mortar. Position the level over more than one slab (place it on a straight-edged piece of wood if necessary).

6 Use spacers of an even thickness to ensure regular spacing. Remove these later, before the joints are filled with mortar.

7 A day or two after laying the paving, go over it again to fill in the joints. Use a small pointing trowel and a dryish mortar mix to do this. Finish off with a smooth stroke that leaves the mortar slightly recessed. This produces an attractive, crisp look. Wash any surplus mortar off the slabs before it dries.

Paving materials

There are plenty of paving materials from which to choose, so spend time looking through brochures and visit garden centres and builders' merchants before you come to a decision.

RIGHT: *Bricks, unlike clay pavers, are laid with mortared joints. This can emphasize the design.*

PAVING SLABS
Rectangular paving slabs

The majority of paving slabs are based on a full-sized slab 45 × 45cm (18 × 18in) or 45 × 60cm (18 × 24in). Half and quarter slabs may be a little smaller in proportion to allow for mortar joints. Thickness may vary according to make, but provided you mix only those made by the same manufacturer this won't matter.

A *smooth* surface can be boring, slippery, and a little too much like public paving, but many have a *textured* finish. Textures vary. A riven finish usually looks like natural stone, an exposed aggregate finish has exposed gravel to give a natural-looking non-slip finish.

Slabs imprinted with a section of a larger pattern are usually unsatisfactory in a small area. As quite a large area of paving is usually required to complete the pattern, they only emphasize the space limitations.

Shaped paving slabs

Use shaped slabs with caution. Circular slabs are useful for stepping-stones, but are difficult to design into a small patio. Hexagonal slabs also need a fairly large area to be appreciated. Special half-block edging pieces are usually available to produce a straight edge.

Paved and cobbled finish slabs

Some designs are stamped with an impression to resemble groups of pavers or bricks, some containing as many as eight basket-weave 'bricks' within the one slab. They create the illusion of smaller paving units, and are very effective in a small area.

TOP LEFT: *Slabs like this are particularly useful for a small area because they give the illusion of smaller paving units.*
TOP RIGHT: *Paving slabs with a riven finish look convincingly like real weathered stone.*
MIDDLE LEFT: *Paving slabs will always weather. Pale colours like this will soon look darker, while bright colours will become muted.*
MIDDLE RIGHT: *Hexagonal paving slabs can be attractive, but are not usually satisfactory in a very small area.*
BOTTOM: *Rectangular shapes like this can be used alone, or integrated with other sizes to build up an attractive design.*

Planting circles

A few manufacturers produce paving slabs with an arc taken out of one corner. Four of these placed together leave a circular planting area for a tree or other specimen plant.

BRICKS AND PAVERS

Bricks and pavers are especially useful for a small garden. You can create an attractive design even in a small area, and you may be able to obtain them in a colour and finish that matches your home, which will produce a more integrated effect.

Always check that the bricks are suitable for paving, however, as some intended for house building will not withstand the frequent saturation and freezing that paths and patios are subjected to. After a few seasons they will begin to crumble. Clay pavers, on the other hand, have been fired in a way that makes them suitable for paving. Concrete pavers and blocks are another option, though these are usually more suitable for a drive than a small patio.

Rectangular pavers

Clay pavers look superficially like bricks but are designed to lock together without mortar. They are also thinner than most bricks, though this is not obvious once they have been laid. Concrete pavers or paving blocks are laid in a similar way and are more attractive than concrete laid in-situ for a drive. They can look a little 'municipal'.

Interlocking pavers and blocks

Concrete pavers or blocks are often shaped so that they interlock. Interlocking clay pavers may also be available.

Bricks

Bricks require mortar joints – they won't interlock snugly like clay pavers. On the other hand you may be able to use the same bricks for raised beds and low walls, giving the whole design a more planned and well-integrated appearance.

To use bricks economically, lay them with their largest surface exposed, not on edge. This excludes the use of pierced bricks (which have holes through them). It does not matter if they have a frog (depression) on one side, provided this is placed face-down.

Setts and cobbles

Imitation granite setts, which are made from reconstituted stone, and cobbles, which are natural, large, rounded stones shaped by the sea or glaciers, are both excellent for small areas of irregular shape. Their size makes them much easier to lay to a curve. Bed them into a mortar mix on a firm base.

Tiles

Quarry and ceramic tiles are appropriate for small areas near the house, or to create a patio that looks just that little bit different. Always make sure ceramic tiles are frostproof. Lay them on a concrete base that has been allowed to set, and fix them with an adhesive recommended by the supplier or manufacturer.

LEFT: *Hard paving comes in many forms. The top row shows (from left to right) natural stone sett, clay paver, clay brick, artificial sett. The centre row shows a typical range of concrete paving blocks. The bottom row illustrates some of the colours available in concrete paving slabs.*

Paths and path materials

As with any other garden structure, paths should be designed to suit the purpose they are to serve. There are a wide range of materials on the market to suit every need so shop around before deciding which you require.

Practical paths should be functional first and attractive second. Drives for cars and paths to the front door must be firmly laid on proper foundations. And don't skimp on width – it is extremely frustrating for visitors if they have to approach your door in single file. It might be better for the route to take a detour, perhaps forming an L-shape with the drive, if there isn't enough space for a wide path directly to the door.

Internal paths, used to connect one part of the garden to another, can be more lightly constructed, and are softened with plants.

Casual paths, which often lead nowhere and are created for effect, such as stepping-stones through a flower bed, can be lightly constructed and much less formal in style.

RIGHT: *Although the gaps between these paving slabs have been filled with chipped bark in this example, you could also use gravel.*

BELOW: *Paving can reflect artistic ambitions.*
BELOW RIGHT: *Victorian-style rope edging.*

Bricks and pavers
These are ideal materials for internal garden paths that have to be both practical and pretty. Complex bonding patterns are best avoided unless the path is very wide.

Paving slabs
By mixing them with other materials the look of paving slabs can be much improved. A narrow gravel strip either side can look smart, and the gravel can be extended between the joints to space out the slabs. The slab-and-gravel combination is ideal if you need a curved path.

A straight path can be broken up with strips of beach pebbles mortared between the slabs. Tamp them in so that they are flush with the surrounding paving.

Crazy-paving

Use this with caution. In the right place, and using a natural stone, the effect can be mellow, and harmonize well with the plants. Be more wary of using broken paving slabs – even though they are cheap. Coloured ones can look garish, and even neutral slabs still look angular and lack the softness of natural stone.

Path edgings

Paths always make a smarter feature with a neat or interesting edging. If you have an older-style property, try a Victorian-style edging. If it is a country cottage, try something both subtle and unusual, like green glass bottles sunk into the ground so that just the bottoms are visible. Or use bricks: on their sides, on end, or set at an angle of about 45 degrees.

CREVICE PLANTS

Plants look attractive and soften the harsh outline of a rigid or straight path. They are easy to use with crazy-paving or any path edged with gravel. It may be necessary to excavate small holes. Fill them with a good potting mixture. Sow or plant into these prepared pockets.

Some of the best plants to use for areas likely to be trodden on are chamomile, *Thymus serpyllum* and *Cotula squalida*. For areas not likely to be trodden there are many more good candidates, such as *Ajuga reptans* and *Armeria maritima*.

HOW TO LAY CLAY OR CONCRETE PAVERS

The method of laying clay or concrete pavers described in the following steps can be used for a drive or a patio as well as a path.

1 Excavate the area and prepare a sub-base of about 5cm (2in) of compacted hardcore or sand and gravel mix. Set an edging along one end and side first, mortaring into position, before laying the pavers.

2 Lay a 5cm (2in) bed of sharp sand over the area, then use a straight-edged piece of wood stretched between two height gauges (battens fixed at the height of the sand bed) to strike off surplus sand and provide a level surface.

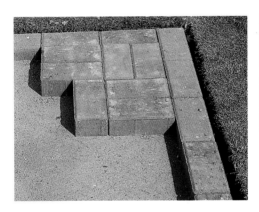

3 Position the pavers, laying 2m (6½ft) at a time. Make sure they butt up to each other, and are firm against the edging. Mortar further edging strips into place as you proceed.

4 Hire a flat-plate vibrator to consolidate the sand. Alternatively, tamp the pavers down with a club hammer over a piece of wood. Do not go too close to an unsupported edge with the vibrator.

5 Brush more sand into the joints, then vibrate or tamp again. It may be necessary to repeat this once more.

Decorative floors

A single surface of one kind of paving is likely to look flat and dull in anything but the smallest of patios. To create a much more interesting view, you might like to introduce some variation and texture – either with different decorative paving materials, or by using plants.

Often, it simply is not practical to go for major change, and you may feel you are stuck with a stretch of uniform concrete slabs. But there are ways to improve the situation – perhaps by removing some of the slabs to increase the planting areas around the perimeter and within the main paving areas. Or you could use decorative detailing to disguise parts of a less than pretty surface.

Ornamental paving
Coloured tiles have been used to create decorative floors down the centuries. It is likely that tiles laid in an intricate mosaic pattern over the whole patio will be overpowering, especially in a very small garden, and put up fierce competition with the plants. However, you can turn an ordinary paved area into something quite distinctive by replacing one or two of the paving slabs with panels of different coloured ceramic tiles. Arrange them in geometric patterns, forming squares, oblongs, or triangles, depending on the layout of the rest of the space. If you have the room you could extend the paved area by adding two rows of tiles around the perimeter; lay them diagonally in alternating colours – perhaps one row in terracotta, the other in cream, again depending on the design of the rest of the paving.

Pebbles
Pebbles are another decorative material with a centuries-old tradition. Their natural colours and smoothly rounded forms can be used to make exquisite textural panels within concrete or brick paving. Again, geometric shapes are most commonly seen but, in the hands of an artist given enough space, they can become elaborate works of art.

Floor planting
One way of softening uninspired areas of large concrete paving is to replace some of the slabs with mini-gardens. Try planting a miniature herb lawn that releases its aroma as you brush past. Chamomile (the non-flowering variety 'Treneague') and thyme are particularly effective. Or you can plant with larger herbs, such as lavender or sage. Low-growing flowers, such as alyssum, violets, pinks or any of the alpines, can offer a subtle but effective splash of floor-level colour.

If the ground allows, you can encourage small plants to grow between the paving stones, but you will need to be selective. While self-seeded violas can look enchanting, thistles are not so appealing.

ABOVE: *This ceramic sun makes an original floor feature. Planted with low-growing plants, it looks like a rich green tapestry.*

BELOW: *The clay-tiled floor and brick retaining walls make an evocative home for a herb garden and a focal point within the garden.*

Gravel beds

Gravel can be used as a straight substitute for grass and requires much less maintenance. You can even convert an existing lawn very simply by applying a weedkiller to the grass, laying edging blocks around the edge, then topping up with gravel.

Informal gravel beds still require some kind of edging restraint to prevent the gravel from spreading. If the bed is surrounded by a lawn, simply make sure that the gravelled area is about 5cm (2in) below the surrounding grass.

Other practical ways to prevent the gravel from scattering onto beds and other unwanted areas are to create a slightly sunken garden or to raise the surround slightly with a suitable edging.

Informal gravel areas often look especially effective if some plants are grown through the gravel – either in beds with seamless edges where the gravel goes over them, or as individual specimen plants.

HOW TO LAY A GRAVEL BED

1 Excavate the area to the required depth – about 5cm (2in) of gravel is sufficient in most cases.

2 Level the ground. Lay heavy-duty black polythene or a mulching sheet over the area. Overlap strips by about 5cm (2in).

3 Then tip the gravel on top and rake level.

4 To plant through the gravel, draw it back from the planting area and make a slit in the polythene. Plant normally, enriching the soil beneath if necessary.

5 Firm in and pull back the polythene before re-covering with gravel.

Forming Boundaries

MOST OF US HAVE AN INSTINCTIVE DESIRE TO mark our territory with a very visible boundary. It gives us a sense of privacy and the illusion of security, but above all it marks out our plot of land, the area in which we create our own very special paradise.

The problem with a small garden is that the boundary forms a large part of the garden, and the chances are that you will see it from whichever direction you look. In a large garden the boundary often merges into the background, but in a small one it can easily dominate.

Tall walls can be an asset – the walled town garden has many of the treasured attributes of an old walled country garden – but drab wooden fences and large overgrown hedges pose real problems if you want to make your garden look smart and stylish.

Don't take your boundary for granted, and never assume it can't be improved. Replacing a fence or grubbing up a long-established hedge are not projects to be tackled lightly – they can be expensive or labour-intensive. Never make changes until you have consulted neighbours that

LEFT: *This is an excellent example of a combination boundary – a wooden picket fence supported on a low wall, with an escallonia flowering hedge growing through it.*

OPPOSITE ABOVE: *Walls make secure boundaries, but to prevent them looking oppressive cover with climbers, and if possible create a view beyond, as this attractive gate has done.*

OPPOSITE: *A wall as tall as this can easily dominate a small garden, but by treating it boldly and using it as a feature it becomes an asset.*

are affected. The boundary may belong to them, in which case it is not yours to change unilaterally. Even if it is legally yours to replace, the courtesy of discussing changes with others affected will go a long way to helping you remain on good terms with your neighbours.

Although you are unlikely to want to exceed them in a small garden, there may be legal limitations on boundary height, perhaps laid down in the terms of the contract when you bought the property. In some countries there may be restrictions placed by the highways authority on road safety grounds.

Restrictions are most likely in front gardens – some 'open plan' estates, for example, may have limitations on anything that might infringe the integrated structure of the gardens.

None of these restrictions need inhibit good garden design, but it is always worth checking whether any restrictions exist before erecting or planting a new boundary.

Hedges for small gardens

Many of the classic hedges, like beech, yew, and tall conifers like × *Cupressocyparis leylandii*, and even the privet (*Ligustrum ovalifolium*) have strictly limited use in a small garden. In small gardens the emphasis should be on plants that have much to offer or compact growth. The hedges suggested here are just some of the plants that could be used to mark your boundary without being dull or oppressive. Be prepared to experiment with others.

Clipped formality

The classic box hedge (*Buxus sempervirens*) is still one of the best. It clips well and can be kept compact, but choose the variety 'Suffruticosa' if you want a really dwarf hedge like those seen in knot gardens. A quick-growing substitute is *Lonicera nitida*, and there's a golden form that always looks bright – but be prepared to cut frequently. Some of the dwarf berberis stand close clipping – try the red-leaved *Berberis thunbergii* 'Atropurpurea Nana'. Yew (*Taxus baccata*) is also excellent for formal clipping, and it can be kept compact enough for a small garden.

Colourful informal hedges

If you want to cut down on clipping, and want something brighter and more colourful than most foliage hedges, try the grey-leaved *Senecio* 'Sunshine' or the golden *Philadelphus coronarius* 'Aureus' (unfortunately sheds its leaves in winter). *Viburnum tinus* can also be kept to a reasonable height, and provided you avoid pruning out the new flowers it will bloom in winter. Many of the flowering and foliage berberis also make good 'shrubby' hedges. These will lack a neatly clipped profile, but pruning and shaping is normally only an annual job.

ABOVE: *Although* Lonicera nitida *needs frequent clipping, it makes a neat formal hedge.*

LEFT: *Many shrub roses can make an attractive flowering hedge in summer, but do not plant them too close to the edge of a path otherwise their thorny stems may be a nuisance.*

HOW TO LAY BRICKS AND BLOCKS

Although bricks are being laid here, the same principles apply to laying walling blocks.

1 All walls require a footing. The one shown here is a for a low wall just one brick wide: for larger and thicker walls the dimensions of the footing will have to be increased.

Excavate a trench about 30cm (12in) deep, and place about 13cm (5in) of consolidated hardcore in the bottom. Drive pegs in so that the tops are at the final height of the base. Use a spirit-level to check levels.

2 Fill with a concrete mix of 1 part cement, 2½ parts sharp sand and 3½ parts 2cm(¾in) aggregate, and level it off with the peg tops.

3 When the concrete has hardened for a few days, lay the bricks on a bed of mortar, also place a wedge of mortar at one end of each brick to be laid. For stability, always make a pier at each end, and at intervals of about 1.8–2.4m (6–8ft) if the wall is long. Here two bricks have been laid crossways for this purpose.

4 For subsequent courses, lay a ribbon of mortar on top of the previous row, then 'butter' one end of the brick to be laid.

5 Tap level, checking constantly with a spirit-level.

6 The wall must be finished off with a coping of suitable bricks or with special coping sold for the purpose.

Boundary fences

Fences have the great merit of being more instant than hedges and less expensive than walls. That is the reason they are so often chosen by builders for new properties, and why they are frequently chosen again when the original fences come to the end of their useful life.

Closeboard and panel fences are popular, but predictable and a little boring. There are plenty of styles to choose from, however, so select a fence appropriate to your garden design yet practical for the purposes you have in mind.

If you want privacy or animal-proofing, you will have to opt for one of the solid styles, but if it is just a boundary-marker that is needed there are many attractive fences that look stylish and won't appear oppressive in a small garden.

The names of particular fence types can vary from country to country. If you do not recognize any of the names here check with the illustrations.

Closeboard

Closeboard fencing is erected on site by nailing overlapping feather-edged boards to horizontal rails already secured to stout upright posts. It is a strong, secure fence, but not particularly attractive – especially viewed from the side with the rails.

Panels

Prefabricated panels are quick and easy to erect and a popular choice for that reason. Panels are usually about 1.8m (6ft) long and range in height from about 60cm (2ft) to 1.8m (6ft), generally in 30cm (1ft) steps. The interwoven or overlapping boards are sandwiched between a frame of sawn timber. The woven style is not as peep-proof as overlapping boards.

Interlap or hit-and-miss

This combines strength and a solid appearance with better wind-filtering than a solid fence (which can create turbulent eddies that can be damaging

ABOVE: *Closeboard fencing well covered with climbing roses.*

ABOVE: *Wattle or woven fences make an attractive background for plants.*

ABOVE: *A low wooden fence is not obtrusive and can look very attractive.*

to plants). It is constructed from square-edged boards that are nailed to the horizontal rails on alternate sides. Overlapping the edges gives more privacy, while spacing them

further apart can look more decorative.

Picket

Picket fences look good in country gardens, but can also be a smart choice for a small town garden. Narrow, vertical pales are nailed to horizontal timbers, spaced about 5cm (2in) apart. You can make them yourself or buy kits with some of the laborious work done for you. The simplest shape for the top of each pale is a point, but you can make them rounded or choose a more ornate finial shape. A picket fence can be left in natural wood colour, but they look particularly smart painted white. Because they are usually relatively low, and you can see plenty of garden through the well-spaced pales, they don't dominate the garden in the same way as a tall, solid fence.

Ranch-style

Ranch-style fences consist of broad horizontal rails fixed to stout upright posts. They are usually quite low, and frequently consist of just two or three rails. White-painted wood is a popular material, but wipe-down plastic equivalents are very convincing and easy to maintain. For a small garden

they provide a clear boundary without becoming a visual obstruction. Also, rain and sun shadows are not created in the way that occurs with more solid fences.

Post and chain

This is the least obtrusive of all fences. Purely a boundary marker, it will do nothing to deter animals or children, or keep balls out of the garden, but it is a good choice if you want a fence that is hardly noticeable. You can use wooden, concrete or plastic posts and metal or plastic chains. Choose a white plastic chain if you want to make a feature of the fence, black if you want the chain to recede and blend into the background.

Chain link

Chain link is not an aesthetic choice, but it is highly practical and an effective barrier for animals. It is probably best to have a contractor erect a chain link fence, as it needs to be tensioned properly. You may like the fact that you can see through it, especially if the view beyond is attractive, but you may prefer to plant

climbers beside it to provide a better screen. Choose tough evergreens such as ivy if you want year-round screening.

Bamboo

Bamboo is a natural choice if you've created an oriental-style garden, but don't be afraid to use this type of fence for any garden style if it looks right. Bamboo fences come in many shapes and sizes, and the one you adopt will depend partly on the availability and cost of the material and partly on your creativity and skill in building this kind of fence.

ABOVE: *A fence like this just needs a supply of bamboo and skill at tying knots!*

LEFT: *A white picket fence can make the boundary a feature of the garden.*

How to erect a fence

Many gardeners prefer to employ a contractor to erect or replace a fence. They will certainly make lighter work of it with their professional tools for excavating post holes, and a speed that comes with expertise, but some fences are very easy to erect yourself. Two of the easiest are panel and ranch-type fences, which are illustrated in simple steps below.

HOW TO ERECT A PANEL FENCE

1 Post spikes are an easier option than excavating holes and concreting the post in position. The cost saving on using a shorter post and no concrete will go some way towards the cost of the spike.

Use a special tool to protect the spike top, then drive it in with a sledge-hammer. Check periodically with a spirit-level to ensure it is absolutely vertical.

2 Once the spike has been driven in, insert the post and check the vertical again.

3 Lay the panel in position on the ground and mark the position of the next post. Drive in the next spike, testing for the vertical again.

4 There are various ways to fix the panels to the posts, but panel brackets are easy to use.

5 Insert the panel and nail in position, through the brackets. Insert the post at the other end and nail the panel in position at that end.

6 Check the horizontal level both before and after nailing, and make any necessary adjustments before moving on to the next panel.

7 Finish off by nailing a post cap to the top of each post. This will keep water out of the end grain of the timber and extend its life.

Brightening up fences and walls

If replacing an existing old fence or wall simply isn't practical because of the time and expense involved, consider ways to camouflage or brighten up the old one.

Climbers

Climbers present one of the most pleasing ways to cover an unsightly wall or fence, but always make sure the fence is firm in its foundations first . . . otherwise the extra weight and wind resistance will just bring it down sooner and you will have to untangle the climber and repair the fence anyway.

For year-round cover, tough evergreens such as ivies are justifiably popular. They can be slow to establish, but ultimately provide dense cover and can easily be clipped back once or twice a year to prevent the shoots encroaching beyond their territory.

For summer-only cover, try the vigorous hop (*Humulus lupulus*), especially in its very attractive golden form 'Aureus'. Once established one plant will cover a large area of fence.

For flowers some of the clematis can be very successful, though winter's an unattractive time. Tall-growing species such as *Clematis montana* sound unlikely candidates, but they will run along the fence and cascade down each side instead of climbing, and the pink *C. m. rubens* looks particularly splendid.

Trained trees

Trained fruit trees can transform a tall wall or fence and turn it into a real feature when laden with flowers or fruit. Even in winter the bare stems of a fan or espalier tree can look dramatic, especially if picked out against a white-painted wall.

Training from scratch is difficult and time-consuming, and it is worth buying ready-trained trees.

RIGHT: *Old fences discolour and look drab and shabby with age. This is one way to transform a dull fence.*

BELOW: *Vigorous clematis such as* C. montana *will cover a fence with blooms in late spring and early summer.*

A coat of paint

A drab old wall can be transformed with a coat of masonry paint. White reflects the light well, but any pale colour can look pleasing, particularly when contrasted with greenery.

Grow striking plants like phormiums or yuccas in front so that their strong profiles are picked out against the background, or stand groups of containers so that they are backed by the painted wall.

Framed effects

Fences are more difficult to paint as a backdrop for plants, and you must be careful about paint seeping through to your neighbour's side, but a little localized painting could work well.

Try a large white circle within which you can frame a striking plant as a focal point. Instead of painting the actual fence, try cutting out a large wooden circle and painting that – then pin it to the fence.

Finishing Touches

A SMALL GARDEN SHOULD BE FULL OF SURPRISES, packed with finishing touches that compensate for the lack of scope offered by limited size.

Many of the focal point techniques used in large gardens can be scaled down and applied on a small scale, and even in a small space the garden can express the owner's sense of fun and personality in the little extras that are grafted onto the basic design.

The whole area can be made to work, every corner can be exploited with devices if not plants, and a degree of flexibility can be built in that makes variety a real possibility.

ABOVE: *A seat like this suggests a gardener with a strong sense of design.*

OPPOSITE ABOVE: *Ornaments have been used to excellent effect here. A sundial commands centre stage and the eye is taken across the garden to a figure which adds light and life.*

OPPOSITE BELOW: *Figures usually look best framed by plants.*

LEFT: *This quiet corner has been transformed by white-painted trellis and a seat.*

ABOVE: *Climbing plants can be grown more horizontally than usual. It is an ideal way to utilize space after the spring flowers have faded.*

ABOVE RIGHT: *A framework of hazel sticks have been woven into an attractive dome. The burgundy clematis that is growing over it is resplendent with flowers.*

RIGHT: *Sweet peas growing up a temporary screen of pea-sticks. Hazel (*Corylus avellana*) is one of the best types of wood, but any finely branched sticks will do.*

ANNUAL CLIMBERS

Asarina
Cobaea scandens (cup-and-saucer vine, cathedral bells)
Eccremocarpus scaber (Chilean glory flower)
Ipomoea (morning glory)
Lablab purpureus (syn. *Dolichos lablab*)
Lagenaria (gourds)
Lathyrus odoratus (sweet peas)
Mina lobata (syn. *Ipomoea lobata*)
Rhodochiton atrosanguineum
Thunbergia alata (black-eyed Susan)
Tropaeolum majus (nasturtium – climbing varieties)
Tropaeolum peregrinum (syn. *T. canariense*) (canary creeper)

Growing climbers through trees

Trees and shrubs make wonderful natural supports for climbers, often providing conditions that are similar to those in the plant's natural habitat. In the wild, particularly in dense woodland or forests, many climbers may grow to 50m (160ft) or more as they grow ever upwards in their search for light, but in the garden supports of this height are rarely necessary – or even available. If they were, the flowers of the climbers using them would be out of sight.

Good partners
Smaller supports are required for cultivated climbers in the garden, and a large apple tree is usually the highest used. Clematis and roses will scramble through its branches, creating huge fountains of flowers. On a more modest scale, even dwarf shrubs can be used to support some low-growing climbers.

Two in one
One of the advantages of growing climbers through shrubs is that it is possible to obtain two focuses of interest in one area. This is particularly valuable for shrubs that flower early, as these tend to be fairly boring for the rest of the year. Through these it is possible to train a later-flowering climber to enliven the area further on in the season. Clematis are particularly good for this, especially the late-flowering forms, such as the viticellas. These can be cut nearly to the ground during winter, so that when the shrub itself is in flower early in the next season, it is relatively uncluttered with the climber.

Roses and fruit
A fruit tree that has come to the end of its fruiting life can be given new appeal if you grow a rose through it. However, it is important to remember that old trees may be weak and the extra burden of a large rose, especially in a high wind, may be too much for it to bear.

BELOW: *Scrambling plants can provide vertical interest through the summer. Here,* Euonymus fortunei *'Emerald Gaiety' scrambles up a tree with* Geranium × oxonianum *below.*

CLIMBERS FOR GROWING THROUGH TREES

Clematis (vigorous kinds)
Hydrangea petiolaris (climbing hydrangea)
Humulus (hop)
Lonicera (honeyuckle)
Polygonum baldschuanicum (syn. *Fallopia baldschuanica*) (Russian vine)
Rosa (roses – vigorous varieties)
Vitis coignetiae (crimson glory vine)

HOW TO GROW A CLIMBER THROUGH A TREE OR SHRUB

1 Any healthy shrub or tree can be chosen. It should preferably be one that flowers at a different time to the climber. Choose companions that will not swamp each other. Here, a low *Salix helvetica* is to be planted with a small form of *Clematis alpina*. The two will make a delicate mix, especially the blue clematis flowers against the silver foliage.

2 Dig the planting area at a point on the perimeter of the shrub and prepare the soil by adding well-rotted organic material. For clematis, choose a position on the shady side of the plant, so that its roots are in shade but the flowers will be up in the sun. Dig a hole that is bigger than the climber's rootball and plant it. Most plants should be planted at the same depth as they were in their pots but clematis should be 5cm (2in) or so deeper.

3 Using a cane, train the clematis into the bush. Once the clematis has become established, you can remove the cane. Spread the shoots of the climber out so that the it spreads evenly through the shrub, not just in one area.

4 If possible, put the climber outside the canopy of the shrub or tree, so that it receives rain. However, it is still important to water in the new plant and, should the weather be dry, continue watering until the plant has become established.

CLIMBERS SUITABLE FOR GROWING THROUGH SHRUBS

Clematis (small varieties)
Cobaea scandens (cup-and-saucer vine, cathedral bells)
Eccremocarpus scaber (Chilean glory flower)
Hedera (ivy)
Ipomoea (morning glory)
Jasminum (jasmine - climbing species)
Lathyrus odoratus (sweet pea)
Lonicera (honeysuckle - climbing species)
Passiflora (passion flower)
Stephanotis floribunda (Madagascar jasmine)
Tropaeolum majus (nasturtium – climbing varieties)
Tropaeolum peregrinum (syn. *T. canariense*) (canary creeper)

Simple pillars

A very effective way of creating vertical emphasis in a border or a small garden is to grow a climber up a single pole, which is usually called a pillar.

Whether solitary or in groups, these can look very elegant and also make it possible to grow a large number of climbers in a relatively small space.

Using pillars

A surprising number of climbers are suited to growing up pillars. Most climbing roses, for example, look particularly good in this situation, although it is probably best to avoid vigorous climbers or rambling roses.

Temporary or permanent

An advantage of using pillars is that they are both inexpensive and simple to erect as well as to take down. They can be permanently positioned in a border, but if you want to be able to remove them in winter, when the plants have died down, set each post in a collar of concrete or a metal tube, so you can simply lift it out when the time comes.

Pillared walkway

If space is available, a very attractive walkway can be created by using a series of pillars along a path. Enhance this further by connecting the tops with rope, along which swags of climbers can grow. This is a delightful way of growing roses and creates a romantic, fragrance-filled route through the garden. The effect is suitable for formal designs, but is so soft and flowing that it gives a very relaxing feel.

CLIMBERS FOR PILLARS

Clematis
Eccremocarpus scaber (Chilean glory flower)
Humulus (hop)
Lonicera (honeysuckle)
Rosa (roses)
Solanum jasminoides (potato vine)
Tropaeolum (nasturtium)

HOW TO MAKE A TREE SEAT

1 Start by securing the legs in position. Use 3.8cm × 7.5cm (1½in × 3in) softwood, treated with a preservative. You will need eight lengths about 68cm (27in) long. Concrete them into position.

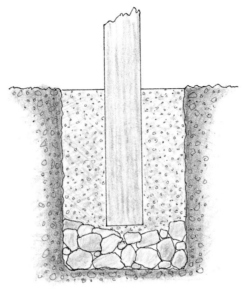

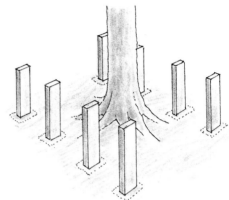

2 Position the legs about 38–45cm (15–18in) apart in two rows about the same distance either side of the trunk.

3 Cut four pieces of 2.5 x 5cm (1 × 2in) softwood for the cross-bars. Allow 7.5cm (3in) over-hang at each end. Drill and screw these to the posts.

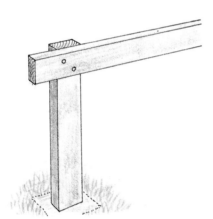

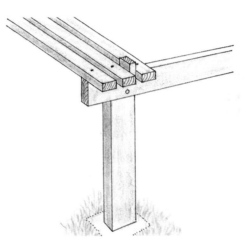

4 Then, cut slats to the required length (the number will depend on the size of your seat). Allow for a 2.5cm (1in) space between each slat. Paint the slats and cross-bars with white paint (or a wood preservative or stain if you prefer), and allow to dry before final assembly. Test the spacing, using an offcut of wood as a guide, and when satisfied that they are evenly spaced on the cross-bars, mark the positions with a pencil. Then glue and nail into position.

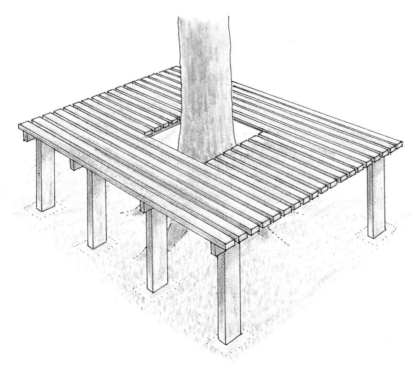

Decorating garden furniture

Co-ordinating furniture with its surroundings helps to give the garden a feeling of harmony. By painting or staining furniture, you can also keep the costs down, as you can pick up bargain pieces from junk shops or rejuvenate old kitchen chairs that are due for replacement. Whether you opt for a simple decorative finish or one that is more elaborate, the key to success lies in the preparatory work you do.

Practicality

If garden furniture is to be left outside all year, bear in mind that any decorative finish will have to be able to withstand a lot of beating from the weather – frosts, strong winds, torrential rain, and the blistering sun of high summer. For this reason, it is best to use exterior-quality products:

they are less likely to peel and flake, their colours are less likely to fade, and they are specifically designed to protect the surface they are covering. However, you can achieve a reasonably hard-wearing finish using paints made for interior use, then finishing with several coats of a polyurethane varnish.

Compatibility counts

Whatever you plan to paint or stain, it is important to use compatible primers, undercoats and varnishes, otherwise they may react against each another. So, if you intend to use a water-based product, make sure that you also prime and finish using water-based products; similarly,

ABOVE: *This colourful, plastic-covered chair offers indoor comfort outside. Its bright green framework and pink floral pattern provide a witty contrast to the Louis XIV style.*

LEFT: *An old Lloyd loom chair has been given a fresh look with two vivid shades of blue spray-on car paint.*

ABOVE: *Clashing Caribbean colours in pink and tangerine make for a lively look in a brightly coloured garden.*

ABOVE: *This simply shaped chair has been given a bright, modern finish to team with the painted shed behind.*

ABOVE: *The same chair has been decorated with a traditional Tyrolean design. The colours complement the colours of a summer garden.*

acrylics should be kept together and oil-based products should be kept together.

Also, ideally, you should stick to one manufacturer's products for each job as that will ensure compatibility. When you are not able to do this, it would be wise to test a small, hidden area first to see how the different products behave.

Working outdoors

If you have to paint outdoors, it is a good idea to choose a dry, warm day – preferably after several similar days and with the prospect of more to come. The reasons for this carefulness are clear. If the surface is damp, the paint will not adhere properly. If the surface is hot, from baking sun, it will blister. If frost is about, it will 'lift' the paint.

Preparatory work

It really is important to make sure the surface you are working on is properly prepared first, following the instructions given by the manufacturer of the product you are using.

Smooth wood

Most garden furniture is made from smooth-planed wood. There are three types of product you can use to paint these: exterior gloss, exterior woodstain, and exterior varnish, which comes in a clear, matt or gloss finish as well as in a wide selection of colours. Most woodstains – as the name implies – come in wood colours, although some specialist manufacturers produce coloured stains too. Garden furniture is usually bought ready-treated with a preservative that you can simply paint over. However, check this is the case before you buy.

Wash the surface with a proprietary paint cleaner or a mild detergent, then rinse thoroughly. Rub down with wet and dry paper. Allow to dry out completely, then paint on a coat of exterior primer. Allow to dry, then rub down and apply an undercoat. Allow to dry, then rub down and apply exterior gloss paint. Always allow plenty of drying time between each stage, taking the manufacturer's specified time as the minimum.

If you would prefer a finish that allows the grain of the wood to show through, you can choose either a woodstain or a varnish. The colour in woodstains penetrates the wood; varnish, even if it is a stained varnish, sits on top. These products are usually applied directly to the clean, dry wood.

Metal

Metal tables and chairs (as well as gates and railings) can be painted with exterior-quality gloss paint. Brush previously painted metal with a wire brush to clean it and remove any loose paint and metal badly eroded by rust. Then dust off. Treat rust with a rust cure and prime any new or bare metal with the appropriate metal primer, then allow to dry before applying the top coat. There are also special metal paints available in aerosol and brush-on versions that can be applied straight over the metal without priming, even if truly rusty. However, it is worth removing any loose rust first with a wire brush.

Entertaining outdoors

Entertaining friends in the garden is one of the joys of summer. Pleasant company and beautiful surroundings rarely fail to induce a feeling of well-being and relaxation, and serving food that you have grown yourself brings deep satisfaction.

The food can be simple, with freshly picked salads, fruits or vegetables and meat or fish grilled or barbecued with fresh herbs, the aroma complementing the scent of the herbs growing in the nearby beds.

ABOVE: *Lunch taken outside in the summer can be a memorable occasion. Attractive garden furniture and a pretty flower arrangement create a suitably restful ambience for eating outdoors.*

However informal the occasion, your guests will feel more comfortable if the eating area is sheltered, rather than completely in the open. If it is not next to the house, it will need to be screened by hedges or trellis to lend some privacy. You don't need a large space – just think how cramped restaurants can be, yet, once seated, you feel comfortable.

Awnings and umbrellas

Shade and shelter are important, but they needn't be permanent fixtures. You can put up a capacious sun umbrella or a prettily striped awning to provide temporary shade – allowing you to dine outside even in the middle of the day in high summer.

Stimulating the senses

Once the eating area is established, try to incorporate something that stimulates each of the senses. Place a handsome specimen plant within view, or position the chairs to look onto a pleasant vista. Nature will offer plenty to please your ear: summer birdsong, the hum of bees and whisper of trees and shrubs gently stirred by a breeze can be enhanced by the tinkling of wind chimes. A water feature can offer the relaxing sound of a trickling stream.

For fragrance, site plants with richly perfumed blooms near the seating area. Old-fashioned roses are hard to beat or try aromatic lavender and rosemary. Many flowers exude their scent at night. Summer jasmine and tobacco plants (*Nicotiana*) are two favourites. For touch, you can plant a contrast of textures from feathery

CLIMBERS FOR ARBOURS

Clematis (some fragrant)
Hedera (ivy – evergreen)
Humulus (hop – dies back in
  the winter)
Lonicera (honeysuckle – many
  fragrant)
Polygonum baldschuanicum (syn.
  Fallopia baldschuanica) (Russian
  vine – very vigorous)
Rosa (roses – many fragrant)

ABOVE: *In the summer, a couple of potted strawberry plants are transformed into a centre-piece when contained in a wire jug.*

love-in-a-mist (*Nigella*) and shapely ferns to rich succulents. Finally, taste can be stimulated by nearby aromatic herbs or fragrant fruits such as strawberries and blackberries.

ABOVE: *Original Edwardian awnings like this one come with a lightweight metal frame that is easily erected and the awning is slipped over.*

Decorating the table
Decorating the table can be effortless. Outdoor table decorations are the very easiest to put together because they are at their most successful when they complement their surroundings. So plunder the garden and then combine the ingredients with flair. You may cut a few flowers, adding foliage or even fruit and vegetables. Or you may simply gather together some of the smaller pots from around the garden. For an evening meal, add soft lighting, such as provided by candles, and the scene will be enticingly set.

Arbours
An arbour – a simple framework over which climbers are trained to create a shady outdoor room – can provide the perfect setting for entertaining friends. It can be just big enough to take a couple of chairs or bench, but best of all is an arbour large enough

to accommodate a table and several chairs, where you can sit and linger over *al fresco* meals.

Designing an arbour
The structure can be of metal or wood, or the arbour can have brick or stone piers with a wooden roof. The design may be triangular, semi-circular, rectangular or octagonal – any shape, in fact, that fits the site.

Most climbers are suitable for clothing the arbour; but if you do not like bees, it is best to stick to climbers grown for their foliage rather than their flowers.

Solid construction
An arbour may have to remain in place for many years, so make sure you build it well. Take trouble to use timbers treated with preservative (not creosote, which may kill the climbers) and make certain that it is a strong design, well supported in the ground. As with similar structures that are covered in heavy climbers, the wind can wreak havoc on weak construction.

Rock and Water Gardens

ROCK AND WATER FEATURES ADD AN EXTRA dimension to any garden, but imagination is needed to get the best from them in a small area. The vast majority of rock and water plants thrive best in a sunny position, and it may be difficult to find a suitable site in a small garden. If you can't find a spot that is in the sun for at least half the day – and preferably longer – it might be better to choose a water feature that depends less on plants for its effect, and to grow your rock plants in other ways, such as between paving and in raised beds or a gravel garden.

Very small ponds are much more difficult to 'balance' biologically than large ones, and green water is often a problem for much of the year. If the garden is very tiny choose a bubble fountain, wall spout, or container pond instead.

Rock gardens look best on a natural slope or built to look like a natural outcrop of rocks in a large lawn. Most small gardens offer neither opportunity. Combining a rock feature with the pond is often the most satisfactory solution. You can create the raised ground from the soil excavated for the pond.

Rock plants – or alpines if you prefer the label – offer huge scope for an enthusiastic gardener with a passion for plants but without the space to grow many. You can plant dozens in the space taken by just one medium-sized shrub, and even the tiniest garden can be home for hundreds of plants.

Be careful with the choice of water plants. Some irises and rushes are compact, others are rampant and will soon make a take-over bid. There are waterlilies that need deep water and a large surface area, others that will be happy in 23cm (9in) of water and will make do with a much smaller surface area.

TOP: Sedum spurium *'Atropurpureum'*.
ABOVE: *Campanulas – here growing through* Asplenium scolopendrium – *are popular rock plants.*
RIGHT: *This sink garden contains more than half a dozen different plants in less space than a single shrub would normally occupy.*
OPPOSITE: *Raising the edges of this pond has emphasized its role as the centre of attention.*
OPPOSITE ABOVE: *Various species of dianthus do well in a rock garden and always have a special appeal.*

Ponds and water features

Making a pond is very easy nowadays – most flexible liners are strong and long-lasting, and pre-formed pools are as near as you can get to buying an instant pond off the shelf. If you don't have space for a 'proper' pond, make one in a barrel or shrub tub.

If you want to grow plants and keep fish, choose a bright position for your pond, one that receives sun for at least half the day. Avoid overhanging trees, they not only cast shade but shed leaves too, which can pollute the water.

Fountains and cascades

Introduce a cascade if you build a rock garden with your pond. A simple low-voltage submersible pump linking the head of the cascade with a hose is usually adequate for a small cascade with a modest flow of water.

Fountains need a large area of water, otherwise drift will cause a gradual drop in the water level. Be aware that the disturbed surface does not suit waterlilies and some other aquatic plants. A simple bubble or geyser type of jet is often more appropriate than a high, ornate jet in a small garden.

ABOVE: *You don't need a large garden to enjoy the sight and sound of moving water, as this attractive feature shows.*

Wall features

In a courtyard or a basement garden enclosed by walls, a wall fountain is often the best choice. You don't need a great gush of water.

You can fix a spout that pours water into a reservoir at the base of the wall to be recirculated through a hidden pump; alternatively buy one that is self-contained with water simply trickling into an integrated dish beneath the spout.

Miniature ponds

If you've no room for a proper pond, make one in a half-barrel or even a plastic shrub tub. Sink it into the ground, half-sink it into the soil, or have it free-standing, perhaps on a paved area such as the patio. Container ponds are not suitable for fish, but you can grow an interesting small collection of aquatic plants in them, including miniature waterlilies.

HOW TO MAKE A POND USING A LINER

1 Mark out the shape of your pond with a piece of rope, hosepipe or by sprinkling sand. Then remove the grass and excavate the soil to the required depth, leaving a shallow ledge about 23cm (9in) wide at about that depth from the top.

2 Remove the grass or soil around the edge if you plan to pave it. Allow for the thickness of the paving plus a bed of mortar. Check levels and remove extra soil from one side if necessary. The water surface needs to be level to the sides of the pond.

3 Remove sharp stones and large roots, then line the pool with about 1cm (½in) of damp sand – it should stick to the sides if they slope slightly. Use a polyester mat (from water garden specialists) or old carpet instead of sand if the soil is stony.

HOW TO INSTALL A PRE-FORMED POND

1 Transfer the shape of your pool to the ground by inserting canes around the edge. Use a hosepipe or rope to define the shape.

2 Excavate the hole to approximately the right depth, and following the profile of the shelves as accurately as possible.

3 Place a straight-edged piece of wood across the top and check that the edges are level. Measure down to check the depths.

4 Place the pool in the hole and add or remove more soil if it does not sit snugly. Also remove any sharp stones. Check that it is absolutely straight with a spirit-level.

5 Remove the pond and line the shape with sand. Backfill so that the pond shape fits the hole snugly.

6 Run water in from a hose, and backfill and firm again as the water rises. Check the levels frequently as the backfilling often tends to lift the pool slightly.

4 Drape the liner over the hole, anchoring the edges with bricks. Run water into the pool from a hose. As the weight of water takes the liner into the hole, release the bricks occasionally. Some creases will form but are not usually noticeable.

5 Trim the liner, leaving an overlap around the edge of about 15cm (6in), to be covered by the paving.

6 Bed the paving on mortar, covering the edge of the liner. The paving should overlap the edge of the pool by about 3cm (1in). Finish off by pointing the joints with mortar.

How to plant a pond

The best time to plant a pond is between mid spring and early summer, when new growth is vigorous yet the plants are not too large. However, most plants can be introduced either earlier or later. Tender floaters such as *Eichhornia crassipes* and *Salvinia braziliensis* should not be introduced while there is a reasonable risk of frost.

HOW TO PLANT WATERLILIES

1 Waterlilies and other deep-water plants can be planted in the same mesh baskets used for marginal plants, but for the more vigorous waterlilies an old washing-up bowl provides more root-run. Plant as for marginals (see below).

2 Cover the soil surface with gravel. There may be space to insert a few oxygenating plants around the edge. These will probably spread and root elsewhere, but it will get them off to a good start.

3 Lower the bowl into the water. If planting early, before the leaf stalks are long, rest the bowl on a couple of bricks for a week or two, then lower to its final position. Different varieties should be planted at different depths.

HOW TO PLANT MARGINALS

1 Use a pond planting basket, and line it with a piece of hessian (sometimes sold for the purpose by water garden specialists) or a piece of horticultural fleece. Fill the container with a soil for aquatics. Insert the plant and carefully firm the soil around the roots.

2 Cover the surface with gravel. This will help to protect the soil from erosion and fish are less likely to stir it up. Gently lower the basket into the water so that it sits on the marginal shelf with about 5cm (2in) of water above the soil.

Six of the best marginals
- *Caltha palustris*
Yellow flowers in spring.
- *Houttuynia cordata*
Small white flowers in summer. Green leaves with red stems, but 'Chameleon' has multicoloured foliage.
- *Iris laevigata*
Mainly blue, white or pink flowers, depending on variety, in summer.
- *Juncus effusus* 'Spiralis'
Stems spirally twisted like corkscrew.
- *Pontederia cordata*
Spikes of pale blue flowers in summer and autumn.
- *Scirpus* 'Zebrinus'
Leaves transversely banded white and green.

- *Hypericum olypicum*
- *Iberis sempervirens* 'Snowflake'
- *Oxalis adenophylla*
- *Phlox douglasii*
- *Phlox subulata*
- *Pulsatilla vulgaris*
- *Raoulia australis*
- *Saxifraga* (mossy type)
- *Sedum spathulifolium* 'Cape Blanco'
- *Sedum spurium*
- *Sempervivum* (various)
- *Silene schafta*
- *Thymus serpyllum* (various)
- *Veronica prostrata*

LEFT: Sempervivum ballsii.

HOW TO PLANT ALPINES

1 Position the plants while still in their pots so that you can see how they look and can move them around easily if necessary.

2 Use a trowel to take out a hole a little larger than the root-ball. You can buy narrow trowels that are particularly useful for planting in the crevices between rocks.

3 Make sure the plant is at the correct depth, then trickle gritty soil around the roots and firm it well.

4 Finish off by covering the exposed surface with more grit.

Choosing Plants

Hard landscaping (paving, walls, fences, pergolas, and so on) is what gives a garden a strong sense of design, and provides the skeleton that gives the garden its shape. But it is the soft landscaping – the plants – that provides the flesh, texture and character of the garden. The same basic design can look very different in the hands of gardeners with different ideas on the use of plants.

ABOVE: *Mixing different types of plant can be very effective. This border contains shrubs, herbaceous plants and bulbs.*

OPPOSITE: *No matter how attractive the structure of a garden, it is the plants that make it pretty.*

Beds and Borders

BEDS AND BORDERS NEED TO BE PLANNED. THE shape will affect the overall appearance, of course, but there are also practical considerations such as the amount of maintenance required, the theme to be created, as well as the crucial question of the actual plants to be used.

Formal beds and borders are normally dictated by the basic design concept, which will often determine the type of plants you can use. A formal rose garden will clearly feature roses, and only the 'filler' plants might have to be debated. A classic style with neat symmetrical beds cut into the lawn, or edged by clipped box, demands the type of formal bedding associated with this type of garden.

Herbaceous and shrub borders are much more open to interpretation, and the actual plants used will have as much affect on the overall impression created as the shape or size of the border.

In traditional large gardens there is a clear distinction between herbaceous borders and shrub borders, but few small gardens can afford this luxury and the inclusion of a 'mixed border' is the usual compromise. Here shrubs jostle for

LEFT: *By curving the corners of borders in a small garden you can generate extra planting space that helps to make the garden more interesting.*

OPPOSITE ABOVE: *A garden like this, with plenty of shrubs such as roses, require little maintenance and because the hard landscaping is minimal is relatively inexpensive to create.*

OPPOSITE BELOW: *Single-sided herbaceous borders can look right in a rural setting if you have enough space. A border like this can be colourful for many months.*

How to get a neat edge

Emphasize the profile of your beds and borders, as well as your paths, by giving them a crisp or interesting edge. A mowing edge is a practical solution for a straight-edged border. Curved beds and borders usually have to be edged in other ways.

Some methods, like the corrugated edging strip and the wooden edge shown below are not particularly elegant, but they help to prevent the gradual erosion of the lawn through constant trimming and cutting back, and they maintain a crisp profile.

Using ornate or unusual edgings

For a period garden, choose a suitable edging. Victorian-style rope edging tiles are appropriate. If you live in a coastal area, consider using large seashells. If you enjoy your wine as well as your garden, why not put the empty bottles to use by forming an edging with them? Bury them neck-down in a single or double row, with just a portion showing.

TOP: *It is possible to buy a modern version of Victorian rope-edging.*
ABOVE: *Edgings such as this are useful if you want to create a formal or old-fashioned effect.*

HOW TO FIT EDGING STRIPS

Edging strips like this are available in a thin metal, soft enough to cut with old scissors, or in plastic. These strips help stop erosion of the grass through frequent edge clipping and cutting back. Although these may not be the most decorative edging strips, they are quick and easy to fit.

1 Make a slit trench along the lawn edge with a spade, then lay the strip alongside the trench and cut to length. Place the edging strip loosely into it.

2 Backfill with soil for a firm fit. Press the strip in gently as you proceed. Finish off by tapping it level with a hammer over a straight-edged piece of wood.

HOW TO FIT WOODEN EDGING ROLL

Wired rolls of sawn logs can make a strong and attractive edging where you want the bed to be raised slightly above the lawn, but bear in mind that it may be difficult to mow right up to the edge.

1 Cut the roll to length using wire-cutters or strong pliers to cut through the wires, and insert the edging in a shallow trench. Join pieces by wiring them together. Backfill with soil for a firm fit. Make sure that the edging is level, first by eye. Use a hammer over a straight-edged piece of wood to tap it down. Then check the height with a spirit-level. Adjust as necessary.

Planning Borders

THE SECRET OF A SUCCESSFUL BORDER IS PLANNING for a long period of interest. However large a border, it probably will not remain attractive for more than about a month if you plan it only with plants that flower together. Planning should include not only plants that make pleasing associations when flowering, but that look good even out of bloom. Also incorporate plants that flower at different seasons.

The risk of planting a series of plants that bloom at different times is an uncoordinated appearance, with plants in flower dotted about amid a swathe of foliage in varying stages of

ABOVE: *Hydrangeas look good in shrub borders or mixed borders, but the flower colour may vary according to the acidity or alkalinity of the soil.*

LEFT: *Don't be afraid to use a focal point like a birdbath in a border. It will be eyecatching even when the plants are not at their best.*

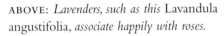
ABOVE: *Lavenders, such as this* Lavandula angustifolia, *associate happily with roses.*

ABOVE: *The fully double, peony-like flowers of* Rosa 'Constance Spry' *are heavily scented.*

Rosa 'Cardinal de Richelieu'
Gallica rose. Compact habit with fully double, deep burgundy-purple flowers in summer *1 × 1.2m (3 × 4ft).*

Rosa 'Constance Spry'
Shrub rose. Arching habit that will climb if supported. Fully double, fragrant, pink flowers in summer *2 × 1.5m (6½ × 5ft)*

Rosa rugosa
Species rose. Wrinkled leaves and cup-shaped flowers in carmine-red from summer to autumn, followed by red to orange-red hips *2 × 2m (6½ × 6½ft).*

neat rounded clumps. Flowers in summer are insignificant. Useful in front of roses *15 × 23cm (6 × 4in).*

Galanthus nivalis
Spring-flowering bulb. This popular bulb often blooms in late winter, otherwise early spring, so use it to provide interest before the roses begin to grow again. The many varieties all have small nodding white bell flowers *10–15 × 5–8cm (4–6 × 2–3in).*

Gypsophila paniculata
Bushy perennial. Small, linear leaves on branching stems, crowned by masses of small white flowers over a long period in summer. *60–90 × 60–90cm (24–36 × 24–36in).*

Hordeum jubatum
Short-lived perennial grass, usually treated as an annual. Arching plume-like flowers spike in summer and early autumn *30–60 × 30cm (12–24 × 12in).*

Lavandula angustifolia 'Hidcote' (syn. *L. spica* 'Hidcote Purple')
Bushy evergreen shrub. Aromatic grey-green leaves and spikes of lilac flowers from mid- to late summer *60 × 75cm (24 × 30in).*

Nepata ×faassenii
Bushy, clump-forming perennial. Small grey-green leaves, topped by

loose spikes of lavender-blue flowers, at their best in early summer. Other bushy species and hybrids are also very suitable for growing with roses *45 × 45cm (18 × 18in).*

Rosa 'Bourbon Queen'
Bourbon rose. Clusters of fragrant, cup-shaped, double, magenta to rose-pink flowers, mainly in summer *2.4 × 1.5m (8 × 5ft).*

Viola × wittrockiana
Biennials, often treated as annuals. Pansies need no introduction, and come in a variety of colours. Some varieties flower mainly in late winter and spring, others in summer *23 × 23cm (9 × 9in).*

BELOW: *This living wall of roses provides a stunning boundary to any garden. Climbing roses quickly give dense cover, providing privacy yet adding a stunning and fragrant attraction to a garden.*

Foliage and grass borders

With the extensive range of flowering plants available, it is easy to overlook the beauty and impact of foliage. Yet many plants are more impressive in leaf than they are in flower, their colours, forms and textures providing interest at various times of year. Foliage plants – whether they be luxuriant ferns, bold hostas, spiky grasses, or fiery maples – are an essential part of any well-planned planting scheme, providing intriguing contrasts and strong architectural impact.

Acer palmatum atropurpureum
Rounded deciduous tree. Stunning red-purple, palm-like leaves that turn red in autumn *8 × 10m (26 × 30ft)*.

Ajuga reptans
Semi-evergreen carpeting plant. Many variegated varieties with multi-coloured leaves. Small blue flowers in summer *10 × 30m (4 × 12in)*.

Alchemilla mollis
Clump-forming perennial. Rounded, crinkly edged pale green leaves, which often hold droplets of dew or rain. Sprays of small greenish-yellow flowers in mid-summer *45 × 45m (18 × 18in)*.

Cortaderia selloana 'Aureolineata'
Evergreen perennial grass. Stiff, arching, yellow-green leaves and silvery yellow plumes on erect stems in late summer *2.2 × 1.5m (7 × 5ft)*.

Bergenia purpurascens
Non-woody evergreen. Large, leathery dark green leaves, turning red in late autumn. Pink flowers in spring *45 × 30cm (18 × 12in)*.

Epimedium perralderianum
Evergreen carpeting plant. Heart-shaped bright green leaves with bronze markings, turning coppery-bronze in winter. Small yellow flowers in early summer *30 × 45cm (12 × 18in)*.

Euonymus fortunei 'Emerald 'n' Gold'
Evergreen shrub. One of several dwarf varieties with attractive variegated foliage, in this case green and gold *60 × 120cm (24 × 48in)*.

LEFT: *A tapestry of greens in high summer, the hosta in the foreground makes its mark long after the spring-flowering daphne and the peony behind have enjoyed their main period of interest.*

BELOW: *This glossy Hosta fortunei var.* hyacinthina *marks a bend in the path. It looks very striking planted with a yellow-leaved berberis.*

Fatsia japonica (syn. *Aralia sieboldii*)
Rounded evergreen shrub. Bold palmate leaves and architectural habit, and small white flowers in autumn, followed by black fruit *2.4 × 2.4m (8 × 8ft)*.

Festuca glauca
Semi-evergreen tufted grass. Bristle-like blue-grey leaves. Small grass flowers in early and mid-summer *15 × 23cm (6 × 9in)*.

Hakonechloa macra 'Alboaurea'
Deciduous grass. Forms clumps of arching narrow golden-yellow leaves from spring till autumn *30 × 30cm (12 × 12in)*.

Heuchera 'Pewter Moon'
Clump-forming perennial. Grey-

marbled, lobed leaves and large, pale pink flowers in early summer *40 × 30cm (16 × 12in).*

Hosta hybrids
Mainly clump-forming perennials. Renowned for their bold foliage that comes in a variety of different shapes and colours such as green, golden yellow, grey-blue or variegated, and for their bell- or funnel-shaped flowers, usually in summer. *H. fortunei* var. *aureomarginata* has yellow-edged, olive-green leaves; *H.* 'Blue Moon' has blue-green foliage; *H.* 'Lemon Lime' is yellow-green; and *H. undulata* var. *undulata* has twisted leaves and white to yellow-white markings *15–100cm × 30–100cm (6–39in × 12–39in),* according to variety.

Matteuccia struthiopteris
Deciduous fern. Erect, pale green fronds resembling shuttlecocks *1.2 × 1m (4 × 3ft).*

Miscanthus sinensis 'Silberfeder' (syn. 'Silver Feather')
Deciduous perennial grass. Downward-arching, pale green leaves with silver midribs and erect silvery plumes in autumn on strong, erect stems *1.8 × 1.5m (6 × 5ft).*

Pennisetum villosum (syn. P. longistylum)
Deciduous perennial grass. Flat or folded leaves and feathery green or

white plumes (purple with age) on arching stems in late summer and early autumn *60 × 60cm (24 × 24in).*

Pleioblastus auricomus (syn. P. viridistriatus)
Evergreen bamboo. Yellow, green-striped linear leaves on hollow, purple-green canes *1.5 × 1.5m (5 × 5ft).*

ABOVE LEFT: Fatsia japonica, *commonly known as the false castor oil plant, has dramatic, rich green leaves that reflect the light.*

ABOVE: *This border contains no flowers, but the impact of the planting comes from dwarf conifers and other foliage plants.*

LEFT: *The leaves of* Hakonechloa macra *'Alboaurea' become tinged with bronze-red along the margins in the autumn.*

Rubus cockburnianus 'Golden Vale'.
Deciduous shrub. Bright golden foliage. The bare thorny stems are attractive in winter, having a white 'bloom' *100 × 100cm (40 × 40in).*

Salvia officinalis 'Purpurascens'
Evergreen or semi-evergreen dwarf shrub. Purple-flushed grey-green leaves. 'Icterina' is grey-green and yellow *60 × 75 m (2 × 2¹/₂ft).*

Stachys lanata (syn. S. byzantina)
Mat-forming, semi-evergreen perennial. Grey-green, furry leaves, with purple-pink flower spikes from early summer to early autumn *45 × 60cm (18 × 24in).*

Colour themes

Colour themes can be very effective, and although it may not be practical to plant whole borders like this in a small garden, you can often use a colour theme in part of a border, devote an island bed to shades of one or two colours, or perhaps cheer up a dull corner with yellow and gold.

Mixed borders

The plants suggested here will form the foundation of a colour theme for a mixed border, but you can add to them and broaden the scope by using bulbs and annuals in appropriate colours too.

Two of the most popular colour ranges are looked at here: blue and silver, and yellow and gold, both of which are ideal for small gardens.

Blue and silver

Agapanthus hybrids
Deciduous to evergreen perennial. Light to deep blue ball-shaped flower heads mid and late summer *45 × 75cm (18 × 30in)*.

Artemisia absinthium
Deciduous sub-shrub. Deeply divided silvery-grey leaves. Yellow flowers in mid and late summer *1m × 60cm (3 × 2ft)*.

Artemisia ludoviciana
Herbaceous perennial. Silver-grey foliage *1m × 45cm (3ft × 18in)*.

Ceanothus x burkwoodii
Evergreen shrub. Clusters of bright blue flowers mid summer to mid autumn *2.4 × 2.1m (8 × 7ft)*.

Delphinium hybrids
Herbaceous perennial. Tall flower spikes in various shades of blue *1.8m × 60cm (6 × 2ft)*.

Festuca glauca
Grass. Dense tufts of blue-grey leaves *23 × 23cm (9 × 9in)*.

Hibiscus syriacus 'Blue Bird'
Deciduous shrub. Lilac-blue flowers late summer to mid autumn *2.4 × 2.4m (8 × 8ft)*.

Nepeta x *faassenii*
Herbaceous perennial. Spike-like heads of lavender-blue flowers all summer. Grey-green leaves *45 × 45cm (18 × 18in)*.

Perovskia atriplicifolia
Shrubby perennial. Feathery sprays of violet-blue flowers in late summer and early autumn. Grey-green leaves *1.2m × 45cm (4ft × 18in)*.

LEFT: *Many ceanothus grow tall, so use them where you need bold plants for the back of a blue border. There are both evergreen and deciduous kinds of ceanothus.*

BELOW LEFT: *Grey-leaved plants are useful for filling in between blue flowers. This one is Artemisia ludoviciana.*

ABOVE: *Delphiniums are some of the best blue herbaceous border plants.*

(30in–20ft × 3–13ft), according to variety.

Phlox paniculata 'White Admiral'
Erect perennial. Fragrant white flowers from summer to autumn *90 × 80cm (36 × 32in)*.

Spiraea 'Arguta'
Rounded deciduous shrub. Small white flowers in spring on arching shoots *2.4 × 2.4m (8 × 8ft)*.

Syringa vulgaris 'Madame Lemoine'
Upright to spreading deciduous shrub. Conical trusses of highly fragrant white double flowers, creamy-yellow in bud, in late spring and early summer *7 × 7m (22 × 22ft)*.

Viburnum plicatum
Deciduous shrub. Large heads of white flowers in late spring and early summer, followed later by red fruits *3 × 3m (10 × 10ft)*.

LEFT: *In the summer the bush* Olearia × haastii *with its daisy-like flowers resembles a miniature snowy mountain. Shown in full flower, this one is delicately fronted by a variegated grass,* Phalaris arundinacea *'Picta'.*

White lilies include *L.* 'Casa Blanca', with bowl-shaped flowers; *L. longiflorum*, which are trumpet shaped; and *L. martagon* var. *album*, with reflexed petals *45cm–2m × 30–60cm (1½–6½ft × 1–2ft)*, according to species or variety.

Olearia × haastii
Bushy evergreen shrub. Daisy-like white flowers with yellow centres from mid- to late summer *2 × 3m (6½ × 10ft)*.

Osteospermum 'Whirligig'
Spreading evergreen subshrub. Highly unusual flowers with spoon-shaped white petals and grey-blue centres *60 × 60cm (24 × 24in)*.

Philadelphus hybrids
Mainly deciduous shrubs. Fragrant white flowers in summer may be single (*P.* 'Belle Etoile'), semi-double (*P.* 'Boule d'Argent') or double (*P.* 'Virginal') *75cm–6m × 1–4m*

ABOVE: *The fragrant white flowers of* Choisya ternata *are produced in profusion in late spring, with some later flowers too.*

ABOVE: Cornus canadensis, *with its starry white flowers, followed by tight clusters of vivid red fruits, is an ideal ground-cover plant.*

Everbright evergreens

Evergreens alone can make a dull garden. They need to be relieved by plants that renew themselves, otherwise you miss the variety that comes with fresh green leaves newly emerged from their buds or the final fling of many shrubs as they go out in a blaze of colourful glory in the autumn. But a garden without evergreens is equally dull, and the clever use of them will ensure that your garden always looks good, whatever the season.

Use a few evergreens in mixed borders and beds, so that there is some height and texture in winter, or devote an area of the garden to evergreens – a heather and dwarf conifer garden can look superb. Try evergreens for focal points and specimen trees in the lawn.

When creating an evergreen bed or border, use plants in many different shades of green, and use variegated plants between plain ones.

Aucuba japonica
Large, glossy leaves. Flowers insignificant, but red berries sometimes a bonus. Choose one of the variegated varieties *1.8 × 1.8m (6 × 6ft)*.

Berberis darwinii
Small, holly-shaped leaves. Masses of attractive small orange-yellow flowers in mid and late spring *2.4 × 2.4m (8 × 8ft)*.

Bergenia hybrids
Evergreen non-woody perennial, useful as ground cover in front of shrubs. Large, rounded leaves, often tinged red or purple in winter. Pink, red or white flowers in spring *30 × 60cm (1 × 2ft)*.

Camellia hybrids
Glossy leaves and large single or double flowers, usually in shades of pink, red or white, in spring *2.4 × 1.8m (8 × 6ft)*.

Ceanothus x *'burkwoodii'*
See *Colour themes*.

Choisya ternata 'Sundance'
See *Colour themes*.

ABOVE: Erica carnea 'Myretoun Ruby' is just one of many attractive winter-flowering plants.

OPPOSITE: *Hebes are excellent compact, rounded plants (though some are tall). This is* Hebe × franciscana 'Variegata', *suitable for even the tiniest plot.*

LEFT: *Evergreens have the advantage of looking good all year, like this combination of* Elaeagnus pungens 'Maculata' *with* Hebe pinguifolia 'Pagei' *in front.*

Cotoneaster dammeri
Prostrate ground cover to use in front of other shrubs. Small leaves. White flowers in early summer, red berries in autumn and winter *5–8cm × 1.5m (2–3in × 5ft).*

Elaeagnus pungens 'Maculata'
Green leaves boldly splashed with gold in the centre. Very striking in winter sun *2.4 × 2.4m (8 × 8ft).*

Erica
There are many species and varieties – look especially for varieties of *Erica carnea* (syn. *E. herbacea*) and *E. x darleyensis*, both winter-flowering and lime-tolerant *30 × 60cm (1 × 2ft).*

Escallonia macrantha
Small leaves, clusters of pink or red flowers in summer *1.8 × 1.8m (6 × 6ft).*

Euonymus fortunei
Will grow along the ground or up against a wall. Choose one of the variegated varieties, such as 'Emerald 'n' Gold' (green and gold) *30cm × 1.2m (12in × 4ft)* on the ground.

Hebe
Hebes make nicely shaped, usually rounded, plants and often have attractive flowers and sometimes colourful or variegated foliage. Heights can range from *30cm–1.2m (12in–4ft)*, with similar spreads, depending on species. Many are of borderline hardiness where frosts can be severe, so check with your local garden centre to see which ones are reliable enough for your area.

Ilex
The holly needs little introduction, but for a small garden choose one trained as a bush and a variegated variety such as 'Golden King' or 'Golden Queen' (the King is female and has berries, the Queen's male and doesn't!) *3 × 2.4m (10 × 8ft).*

Lonicera nitida 'Baggesen's Gold'
See *Colour themes*.

Mahonia 'Charity'
Fragrant clusters of yellow flowers in early and mid winter *2.4 × 1.8m (8 × 6ft).*

Phormium hybrids
Tall, sword-shaped leaves arising from ground level. Usually variegated cream or shades of pink or purple, according to variety. Of borderline hardiness in areas where frosts can be severe, so check with your local garden centre about which ones are suitable for your garden *1.2–1.8m × 1–1.2m (4–6ft × 3–4ft).*

Rosmarinus officinalis
Grey-green, aromatic leaves. Small blue flowers in spring *1.8 × 1.5m (6 × 5ft).*

Santolina chamaecyparissus
See *Colour themes*.

Senecio 'Sunshine'
See *Colour themes*.

BELOW: *Rosemary is pretty in flower, and in mild areas will often start blooming in late winter.*
LEFT: *Hollies are usually so slow-growing that most people can find space for one. This one is* Ilex aquifolium *'Aurea Marginata'.*

Viburnum tinus
Deep to mid green leaves on tidy bush. White flowers (tinged pink in some varieties) from late autumn to early spring *2.4 × 1.8m (8 × 6ft).*

Yucca filamentosa 'Variegata'
Sword-like leaves with broad cream and yellow margins. Large bell-shaped flowers on tall spikes in mid and late summer *1.2 × 1m (4 × 3ft).*

DWARF CONIFERS

A good garden centre will have hundreds of dwarf conifers, in a huge range of shades, shapes, and sizes. The permutations are enormous, and the best way to choose them is to go along armed with a book or catalogue that will give you likely sizes after, say, 15 years, then choose combinations that will make a pleasing group.

Colour for the cold months

Evergreens provide winter clothes for the garden, but they don't look very dressy and they are best interspersed with plants that renew themselves. There is no substitute for flowers and fruits, which, though more transient, are all the more appreciated.

Autumn leaf colour can be as bold and bright as many flowers, but it is worth including some autumn blooms too. A few well-placed pools of late flowers will prolong summer and keep autumn at bay.

Don't overlook colourful barks and twigs in winter, which can become focal points on a sunny day.

Chimonanthus praecox
Deciduous shrub. Scented yellow flowers on bare stems in winter *2.4 × 2.4m (8 × 8ft)*.

Chrysanthemum
Look for varieties that flower late. Some flower well into late autumn and even early winter. Height varies with variety. Consult a specialist book or ask your garden centre for suitable varieties.

Colchicum speciosum and hybrids
Corms with large crocus-like flowers, mainly in shades of pink and mauve, single or double, in autumn. The foliage does not appear until spring *15 × 23cm (6 × 9in)*. The leaves can double the height.

Cornus mas
Deciduous shrub or small tree. Masses of tiny yellow flowers on bare branches in late winter and early spring *3 × 2.4m (10 × 8ft)*.

Crocus speciosus
Corm. Lilac-blue typical crocus flowers in mid autumn *10 × 8cm (4 × 3in)*.

Crocus tommasinianus
Corm, flowering between mid winter and early spring. Typical crocus flowers, usually lilac or purple in colour *8 × 8cm (3 × 3in)*.

Cyclamen coum
Corm. Miniature cyclamen-shaped flowers with reflexed petals. Mainly shades of pink, but also white. Flowers early winter to early spring. Leaves often marbled silver *8 × 15cm (3 × 6in)*.

Cyclamen hederifolium (syn. *C. neapolitanum*).
Similar to above but flowers from late summer to late autumn.

Erica
See *Everbright evergreens.*

Hamamelis mollis
Fragrant spidery yellow flowers on bare branches in mid and late winter *2.4 × 2.4m (8 × 8ft)*.

ABOVE: Chrysanthemum *'Ruby Mound'*.

LEFT: *Long before spring crocuses are in flower, the blooms of* C. tommasinianus *will be putting in an appearance. These were photographed in late winter.*

Helleborus niger
Evergreen perennial border plant.
Large white flowers in mid winter
30 × 45cm (12 × 18in).

Helleborus orientalis
Evergreen perennial border plant.
Large white, pink, or purple flowers
in late winter and early spring *45 ×
60cm (18in × 2ft).*

Iris unguicularis (syn. *I. stylosa*)
Evergreen perennial border plant.
Large blue iris flowers in winter and
early spring *30 × 45cm (12 × 18in).*

Jasminum nudiflorum
Sprawling shrub, usually grown
against a wall or trellis. Bright yellow
flowers from late autumn to early
spring *2.4 × 2.4m (8 × 8ft).*

Mahonia 'Charity'
See *Everbright evergreens.*

Nerine bowdenii
Heads of pretty pink, spidery flowers
on leafless stems from late summer to
early winter. The foliage appears in
spring *60 × 30cm (2 × 1ft).*

Prunus subhirtella 'Pendula' (syn.
'Autumnalis Pendula')
Small to medium-sized drooping
deciduous tree. White flowers,
sometimes tinged pink, from late
autumn and throughout the winter in
mild spells *3 × 3m (10 × 10ft).*

Sternbergia lutea
Bulb. Crocus-like yellow flowers in
mid and late autumn *10 × 10cm
(4 × 4in).*

Viburnum x *bodnantense* 'Dawn'
Deciduous shrub. Small clusters of
white to pink flowers on bare stems
from late autumn to early spring
2.4 × 1.5m (8 × 5ft).

Viburnum tinus
See *Everbright evergreens.*

LEFT ABOVE: *The hellebores span winter and
spring. This is* H. orientalis guttatus.
LEFT: Iris unguicularis *can be in bloom in
mild spells right through the winter. The
plants take a few years to settle down before
flowering prolifically.*
BELOW: Nerine bowdenii *flowers in autumn,
but will sometimes continue into winter.*

COLOURFUL STEMS

A specimen tree with attractive
bark, perhaps placed in a lawn or
in an open position and
surrounded by winter-flowering
heathers, can be a winter focal
point. One of the white-bark
birches such as *Betula jacquemontii*
always looks good. If you need a
really small tree, however, try
B. pendula 'Youngii', a small
weeping tree.

In a small garden, shrubs are
more likely to be a practical
proposition, and two of the best
are *Cornus alba* 'Sibirica' (red
stems) and *C. stolonifera*
'Flaviramea' (green stems).

As a half-way house between
tree and shrub, pollard *Salix alba*
'Chermesina', a willow with
scarlet shoots. Cut the stems
hard back to a stump perhaps
1.2m/4ft tall; do this every
second year.

Autumn leaves and berries

Autumn tints will provide a few extra weeks of border colour at a time when every bit of interest in the garden is appreciated. Berries also add a dash of spice, and some of them will remain for many months, even through to spring in a mild winter when the birds leave them alone.

Amelanchier laevis
A small deciduous tree or large shrub. Masses of white flowers in spring, sometimes black berries in summer, rich autumn foliage colour. *A. lamarckii is very similar 3 × 2.4m (10 × 8ft).*

Berberis thunbergii
Deciduous shrub. Yellow flowers in spring, scarlet berries and brilliant red autumn foliage. *1.2 × 1.5m (4 × 5ft).*

Berberis wilsoniae
Deciduous shrub. Small yellow flowers in mid summer, coral red berries and red and orange foliage in autumn *1 × 1.2m (3 × 4ft).*

Ceratostigma plumbaginoides
Deciduous sub-shrub. Clusters of small blue flowers appear from mid summer to late autumn. Leaves turn red in autumn *30 × 45cm (12 × 18in).*

Clerodendrum trichotomum
Large deciduous shrub. Starry white fragrant flowers in late summer, followed by blue berries in crimson calyces in early and mid autumn *2.4 × 2.1m (8 × 7ft).*

Cornus alba
Deciduous suckering shrub. Attractive autumn foliage colouring, red stems in winter *2.1 × 2.1m (7 × 7ft).*

Cotoneaster horizontalis
Deciduous, ground-hugging shrub for front of border (can also be used against a fence or wall). Small pink flowers in early summer, followed by red berries later. Bright red foliage tints in autumn *60cm × 1.8m (2 × 6ft).*

ABOVE: *The amelanchiers are usually grown for their white flowers in spring, but they have a second burst of colour when the leaves turn. This species is* A. laevis.

LEFT: Cornus alba *is an excellent shrub. After the brief spell of glory as the leaves colour before they fall, there is the winter-long attraction of red stems.*

Fothergilla major
Deciduous shrub. Dark green leaves, orange-yellow or red before they fall. Scented white flowers in late spring *1.8 × 1.5m (6 × 5ft)*.

Ilex
See *Everbright evergreens*.

Malus 'John Downie'
Small to medium-sized deciduous tree. White apple blossom in late spring. Conical yellow and crimson crab apples in autumn *6 × 2.4m (20 × 8ft)*.

Malus tschonoskii
Deciduous tree, which though tall is a candidate for a small garden by virtue of its slender, pencil-like profile. White blossom tinged pink in late spring. Dull red fruits flushed yellow (not a feature). Red and yellow autumn foliage *6 × 2.1m (20 × 7ft)*.

Pernettya mucronata
Evergreen shrub. Small, sharply pointed glossy leaves. Insignificant white flowers in late spring. Clusters of berries – shades of pink, red, purple and white, according to variety – in autumn and winter. Male and female plants must be grown together to ensure fruiting *1 × 1.2m (3 × 4ft)*.

LEFT: *Most sorbus are grown for their red or orange berries, but some also have white or yellow berries, and there is the bonus of spectacular leaf colour just before they fall. This is* Sorbus 'Joseph Rock'.

Pyracantha 'Orange Glow'
Evergreen shrub, usually grown against a wall but also an attractive free-standing plant. White flowers in early summer, orange-red berries in autumn and winter. There are other suitable species and varieties *2.4 × 2.4m (8 × 8ft)*.

Rhus typhina (syn. *R. hirta*)
Deciduous small tree or large shrub. Large, divided leaves, colouring orange-red and yellow before they fall *3 × 3.5m (10 × 12ft)*.

Skimmia japonica
Evergreen shrub. Fragrant creamy-white flowers in spring, red berries in late summer and early autumn. Male plant needed to pollinate female *1 × 1m (3 × 3ft)*.

Sorbus
Many species and hybrids make small or medium-sized trees with red or yellow berries and good autumn foliage colour. Good ones are *S. aucuparia* and hybrids, *S.* 'Embley', and *S.* 'Joseph Rock'.

ABOVE: Pernettya mucronata *is available with pink and red berries as well as white ones. This variety is* 'Mulberry Wine'.
RIGHT: *Skimmias have long-lasting red berries. This one is* S. japonica 'Nymans'.

Variety with variegation

Variegated plants make a border look lighter and more interesting when flowers are scarce, and variegated evergreens are particularly useful at times when little is flowering.

Avoid planting too many variegated plants close together. Use them between other plants with plain foliage where the leaf colouring will be shown off to advantage.

Aralia elata 'Variegata'
Deciduous shrub or small tree. Leaflets margined and marked creamy-white ('Aureovariegata' has a broad, irregular gold margin). White flowers in late summer and early autumn *3 × 2.1m (10 × 7ft)*.

Arundinaria viridistriata (syn. *Pleioblastus auricomus, Pleioblastus viridistriatus*)
Bamboo. Dark green leaves broadly striped yellow. Purplish-green canes *1m × 60cm (3 × 2ft)*.

ABOVE: Hosta fortunei albopicta.
BELOW: *Only a few variegated trees are suitable. This is* Aralia elata *'Variegata'*.

Aucuba japonica (variegated varieties)
See *Everbright evergreens*.

Buxus sempervirens 'Aureovariegata'
Evergreen shrub with small leaves striped, splashed and mottled pale yellow. 'Elegantissima' has irregular creamy-white margins *1.2 × 1m (4 × 3ft)*.

Carex morrowii 'Evergold'
Sedge
Clump-forming with grass-like leaves striped yellow along the centre *25 × 30cm (10 × 12in)*.

Cornus alba 'Elegantissima'
Deciduous suckering shrub with red stems and leaves margined and mottled with white. 'Spaethii' is similar but has gold variegation *2.1 × 1.8m (7 × 6ft)*.

Elaeagnus x *ebbingei* 'Limelight'
Evergreen shrub. Large green leaves with a central splash of deep yellow *2.4 × 2.1m (8 × 7ft)*.

Elaeagnus pungens 'Maculata'
See *Everbright evergreens*.

Euonymus fortunei (variegated varieties)
See *Everbright evergreens*.

Fuchsia magellanica 'Versicolor'
Deciduous shrub. Small fuchsia-type flower in summer and into autumn. Grey-green, white, yellow, and pink variegation. Hardy except in cold areas *1.2 × 1m (4 × 3ft)*.

Hebe x *franciscana* 'Variegata'
Evergreen shrub, not suitable for very cold areas. Small rounded leaves edged cream. Mauve-blue flowers in summer *60 × 60cm (2 × 2ft)*.

PLANTING A CONIFER AND HEATHER MIXED BED

1 Arrange the conifers on the bed first, ensuring they look pleasing from all angles. Move them around in their containers if you are not satisfied at first. Prepare the ground thoroughly, then plant the conifers, firming them in before watering.

2 Space the heathers out around the conifers. Plant in groups or drifts of one variety at a time. Avoid planting too close together, as both heathers and conifers will spread.

BELOW: *A mixed heather and conifer bed will provide interest and at no extra upkeep. Modify the bed to suit the size of your garden and the plants available from your local garden centre.*

3 Apply a mulch of chipped bark or gravel around the plants, to hide the bare soil and make the bed look more attractive.

Maintaining Beds and Borders

Once you have designed and planted a new bed or border, much of the work will be complete. But, no matter how large or small the planting area, there will always be something to do to make it look better, so that it continues to please and delight all who see it.

Immediately after planting, the new border is bound to look bare – and it will remain this way for a while until the roots have become well established and the plants have begun to make some top growth. Applying a mulch – of bark chippings, for example – around the plants will not only make the border look more attractive, it will keep weeds down and help to retain warmth and moisture in the soil. Depending on the material used, the mulch will need to be renewed at least once a year if it is to remain effective.

The plants will need plenty of water at regular intervals, especially throughout the first growing season. Always water thoroughly, as shallow, impatient watering will encourage surface rooting instead of deeper roots, and make the plants even more vulnerable to drought. Try to water in the early morning or late in the day, when the plants are not exposed to full sun, otherwise their leaves may get scorched.

Although many perennials will support their flower stems without any extra staking or supports, some – like the sumptuous large-flowered peonies with their heavy buds and full flowers – will flop onto other plants, especially during a spring shower. Ideally, stakes or supports should be put in place when you are planting the border, even though they may look a little odd at first, when the plants are still small. Failing this, you will need to check regularly that plants aren't being flattened by the weather, or by other plants, and insert supports wherever you can.

Good preparation of the soil should have rid you of deep-rooted and creeping perennial weeds, such as dock and couch grass. Once the border is planted, you will have to remove any fresh growth carefully with a hand fork so you do not damage the border plants. Pull up any annual weed seedlings as soon as you see them – and certainly before they have a chance to flower and shed their seed, otherwise they will simply proliferate and you will have an even bigger problem to deal with next year.

Once they are established, you may want to give your plants an annual feed of a balanced fertilizer, to keep them growing well.

Last, but by no means least, you will need to go through the border regularly, removing flowers as they fade. This will stimulate the plants to produce another crop of flowers, so keeping the border in bloom over as long a period as possible.

LEFT: *This border builds up from the front but is not regimented as the heights vary along its length. It illustrates the effectiveness of using different forms, colours and leaf shapes.*

OPPOSITE: *A good combination of textures, shapes and colours is achieved here with cardoon (Cynara cardunculus) providing interesting structure with pink Salvia sclarea.*

Staking border plants

Some border plants, particularly tall ones, are prone to wind damage, and sometimes a potentially beautiful plant is flattened or broken by the weather. If you stake them early, the plants will usually grow through or over the support, which will then become almost invisible.

1 Proprietary supports like this are very efficient at holding up border plants that are not particularly tall but have masses of floppy or fragile stems.

2 Proprietary supports that link together as shown are useful where you are dealing with clumps of varying sizes. They can be linked together as required.

3 Twiggy sticks pushed into the ground within and around the plant can provide a very effective means of support. Once the plant grows you won't notice them.

4 Short canes can be used to support plants such as carnations. If you use a stout cane, loop string or twine around it as well as the plant. Use thinner split canes to keep individual flower stems or groups of stems upright.

ABOVE: *Mixing materials breaks up a large area of garden and prevents it looking dull. A few of the plants at the back of the border are staked to protect them against adverse weather.*

(usually within 5–7 days), and are useful as a fast-acting tonic if a plant is looking ill. This is especially true of foliar feeds, which are applied directly to the leaves rather than to the soil around the roots, and are absorbed straight into the plant's system. These can have an effect within about 3–4 days, compared with up to 21 days for a general granular fertilizer applied around the roots.

The N:P:K ratio
On the pack of fertilizer, there should be some information about the nutrients it contains. The three most important elements are nitrogen (N), phosphorus (P) and potassium (K). Nitrogen promotes healthy growth of leaves and shoots; phosphorus is needed for healthy root development; and potassium improves flowering and fruit production. Put simply, N:P:K equals shoots:roots:fruits.

The ratio is given on the back of the pack because certain plants need some elements in a greater quantity than others. A foliage plant, for example, will need more nitrogen and less potassium, as it produces leaves but not a great show of flowers or fruit, whereas a fruiting tomato plant needs a huge quantity of potassium to give a good yield.

It is often necessary to change the fertilizer through the season, particularly if you have planted heavy feeders such as vegetables. Apply more nitrogen and phosphorus in the spring to promote growth, and increase the levels of potassium as the season progresses, in order to produce a good show of flowers or fruit.

Applying fertilizer
In an established garden you can apply fertilizer in granular form as a dressing around the plants early in the season, or in soluble form as the plants are watered during the spring. For a new plant, mix fertilizer with the soil as it is replaced in the planting hole around the root-ball.

FEEDING BEDS AND BORDERS

Unless rain is expected, you should water the ground well. This will make the fertilizer active more quickly in dry conditions.

1 Most established plants benefit from annual feeding. Apply a slow- or controlled-release fertilizer in spring or early summer, sprinkling it around the bushes. Sprinkle it further out where most of the active root growth is.

2 Hoe the fertilizer into the surface so that it penetrates the root area more quickly.

3 Unless rain is expected, you will need to water well. This will make the fertilizer active more quickly in dry conditions.

Plants for a Purpose

ONE OF THE SECRETS OF SUCCESSFUL GARDENING IS the ability to choose the right plant for a particular position or use. Plants will always thrive more readily if they are suited to the conditions. Forcing an inappropriate plant into shade if it demands sun, or planting a shade-lover in scorching sunlight, is a recipe for disappointment.

You will find plenty of ideas for plants that relish problem areas like shade or sun in the pages that follow, but sometimes the question is less which plant suits particular conditions as which fulfils a particular purpose. In the following pages you will find plants that provide the right solution, whether you want a scented shrub, climber for a pergola, or an arresting

ABOVE: *Don't be afraid to grow shrubs and plants such as lilies in pots and tubs as well as the more ubiquitous seasonal summer flowers.*

LEFT: *Climbing and rambling roses are useful for summer screens, but bear in mind that it is only seasonal cover.*

LEFT: *Clematis can be planted in shade provided they can rise above it to flower in the sun.*

OPPOSITE ABOVE: *Ivies will grow almost anywhere, in sun or shade, along the ground or up a wall or tree. Green varieties can be a trifle boring, but variegated varieties are always bright.*

BELOW: *'Exotics' can be used as focal points to bring interest to an otherwise boring area during the summer, but will probably need winter protection.*

'architectural' plant as a focal point.

There are 'exotics', some of which are quite tough, other plants will only thrive during the summer months and you will either have to protect them in winter or treat them as expendable. There are also suggestions of plants to attract wildlife.

If a particular variety has been mentioned, other varieties, perhaps in different colours or with minor variations in size or shape, will almost certainly do well in the same situation. White and pale colours tend to show up better in shade, however, and where possible varieties particularly suited to the conditions have been mentioned.

Be prepared to experiment with plants, especially with those that seem to thrive in similar situations in your area, and concentrate on those that clearly do well. Do not be afraid to abandon plants that fail to live up to expectations.

The garden's aspect

The aspect of the garden is something about which you don't have any choice. Whichever direction it faces, however, there will be a range of plants suitable for growing in it. Selecting the right plants will produce a wonderful show of colour throughout the year.

Know your plants

The direction the garden faces will have a strong influence on the plants likely to thrive in it. If a plant originally hails from the warm, dry and sunny countries that border the Mediterranean, it is unlikely to grow well in a damp, shady corner. Similarly, a bog plant from a northern forest will not enjoy being placed between a south-facing wall and a path.

One of the keys to successful gardening is to match the position and the plant as closely as possible. Doing this when the plant is first acquired will save both time and money, because the plant will not have to be dug up later when it has failed to thrive and most of the growing season has been lost. A good nursery is invaluable for advice, but most plants will be labelled with the conditions they prefer.

Plants for 'morning-sun' positions

Berberis darwinii
Bergenia cordifolia
Chaenomeles × superba
Clematis montana
Clematis tangutica
Cotoneaster horizontalis
Deutzia scabra
Dodecatheon meadia
Euphorbia griffithii
Forsythia suspensa
Galanthus nivalis
Hamamelis mollis
Helleborus foetidus
Hypericum 'Hidcote'
Lonicera periclymenum
Pyracantha
Rosa rugosa
Vinca major

BELOW: *Choosing plants with interest in different seasons is vital for a small garden as this* Parthenocissus henryana *shows.*

Plants for shady positions

Akebia quinata
Berberis × stenophylla
Camellia japonica
Camellia × williamsii
Clematis alpina
Clematis 'Nelly Moser'
Choisya ternata
Crinodendron hookerianum
Digitalis
Euonymus fortunei
Garrya elliptica
Hedera colchica
Hedera helix
Hydrangea petiolaris
Ilex
Jasminum nudiflorum
Kerria japonica 'Pleniflora'
Mahonia japonica
Parthenocissus
Piptanthus laburnifolius
Tropaeolum speciosum

PLANTING A FERN BORDER

Ferns are easy to grow as long as they are given the right conditions. Most prefer a moist, shady or partially shady site, and it pays dividends to prepare the ground thoroughly. Spring is a good time to plant.

1 Most ferns need a moist, humus–rich soil, so fork in as much garden compost or rotted manure as possible. This is especially important if the area is shaded by trees, or a wall that also casts a rain shadow, where the soil is usually dry.

2 If the soil is impoverished, add a balanced fertilizer and rake it into the surface. If planting in late summer or winter, do not use a quick-acting fertilizer. Wait until spring to apply, or use a controlled-release fertilizer that will release the nutrients only when the weather is warm enough for growth.

3 It is very important that ferns do not dry out, especially when newly planted. Water the pots thoroughly about half an hour before planting, to make sure the root-ball is wet enough to start with.

4 Make a hole large enough to take the root-ball, but if the roots are very tightly wound round the pot, you will need to carefully tease out some of them first. This will encourage them to grow out into the surrounding soil. If the plant is in a large pot, you may have to use a spade instead of a trowel.

5 Firm in carefully to eliminate any large air pockets that could allow the roots to dry out. Then water thoroughly so that the surrounding soil is moist down to the depth of the root-ball.

6 To help conserve moisture and maintain a high level of organic matter in the soil, mulch thickly with peat moss, leaf mould or garden compost. You will need to freshen the mulch each spring.

Sun lovers

Sunny spots where the ground is moist, or where the sun is intense for just part of the day before it moves around, present no problem for the majority of plants. All except the shade-loving plants are likely to thrive. But if the position is sunny nearly all day, and the soil tends to be free-draining and dry, you need plants adapted to such bright and arid conditions.

Fortunately, those plants that do well in these positions are often bright, floriferous, and very colourful. As a general rule, grey-leaved plants are well suited to these conditions, but if in doubt check.

Most of the plants suggested here tolerate dry soil well. However, give perennials and shrubs extra attention for the first season. Once they get their roots down they should be able to survive happily in a normal year.

Achillea filipendulina
See *Colour themes.*

Agapanthus hybrids
See *Colour themes.*

Alyssum saxatile
See *Colour themes.*

Artemisia arborescens
Semi-evergreen shrub. Silvery-white, much divided leaves. Yellow flowers in early and mid summer. Not reliably hardy in cold areas *1.2 × 1.2m (4 × 4ft).*

Buddleia davidii
See *Planting for quick results.*

Caryopteris x *clandonensis*
See *Planting for quick results.*

Colutea arborescens
Deciduous shrub. Divided, pale green leaves, and yellow pea-like flowers in summer. These are followed by inflated seed pods, flushed coppery-red *2.4 × 2.4m (8 × 8ft).*

Convolvulus cneorum
Evergreen shrub. Silvery foliage. Funnel-shaped white flowers, flushed pink beneath the petals, all summer *60 × 60cm (2 × 2ft).*

Cytisus scoparius hybrids
Deciduous shrub. Green branches make it look evergreen. Pea-type flowers, in shades of yellow, red and pink, many multicoloured, in late spring and early summer *2.4 × 1.8m (8 × 6ft).*

Echinops ritro
Herbaceous perennial. Divided, prickly grey-green foliage, spherical steel blue flower heads in mid and late summer *1m × 60cm (3 × 2ft).*

ABOVE: *Osteospermums thrive in a hot, sunny situation. This one is* O. jacundum.

ABOVE LEFT: Colutea arborescens *has the bonus of interesting inflated seed pods as well as pretty yellow flowers.*

ABOVE RIGHT: Helianthemum nummularium *hybrids thrive in hot, sunny situations. They come in a variety of colours, mainly reds, pinks and yellows.*

OPPOSITE BELOW: Phlomis fruticosa *can be a rather coarse-looking plant, but it thrives in hot, dry soils.*

ABOVE: *Rock roses (Cistus) are fine summer-flowering plants and can cope well with drought.*

ABOVE: *This beautiful biennial* Dianthus barbatus *'Scarlet Beauty' flourishes in chalk.*

LEFT: *The fragrant flowers of lilac (*Syringa*) range from deep pink through mauve to white. This lilac is* S. × vulgaris.

Gypsophila
Semi-evergreen or evergreen perennials and annuals. Clouds of small, star- to trumpet-shaped, white or pink flowers in late spring to autumn *5cm–1.2m × 15cm–1m (2in–4ft × 6–39in)*, according to variety.

Helianthemum nummularium
Evergreen shrub. Pink, red or yellow single or double flowers over grey-green foliage in early and mid summer *15–23 × 60cm (6–9 × 24in)*.

Kolkwitzia amabilis
Erect then drooping deciduous shrub. Abundant clusters of bell-shaped, soft pink flowers in late spring and early summer *3 × 4m (10 × 13ft)*.

Lonicera × brownii (syn. L. sempervirens) 'Dropmore Scarlet'
Deciduous or semi-evergreen climber. Long, trumpet-shaped scarlet flowers in summer *4 × 3m (12 × 13ft)*.

Phlomis fructicosa
Evergreen spreading shrub. Deep yellow flowers in early and mid summer, above grey-green sage-like foliage *1.2 × 1.2m (4 × 4ft)*

Potentilla fruticosa
Deciduous shrub. Dark green leaves and saucer-shaped, bright yellow flowers from late spring to late summer *1 × 1.5m (3 × 5ft)*

Scabiosa 'Butterfly Blue'
Branched perennial. Grey-green leaves and lavender-blue flowers in mid and late summer *40 × 40cm (16 × 16in)*.

Syringa vulgaris
Deciduous shrub. Fragrant single or double flowers, in shades of blue, purple, cream, and white, in late spring or early summer *3 × 2m (10 × 8ft)*.

Verbascum hybrids
Biennials and perennials. Most have tall, slim spires of flowers in summer. *V. chaixii* has felted leaves and yellow flowers with purple centres; *V. chaixii* 'Album' is white with mauve centres; and *V. phoeniceum* is smaller, with clusters of flowers surrounded by leaves *5cm–2m × 15–60cm (2in–6½ft × 6–24in)*, according to variety.

biennials, such as *Dianthus barbatus*. Size depends on species.

Erysimum cheiri (syn. Cheiranthus cheiri)
Bushy evergreen perennial usually treated as biennial. Fragrant single or double flowers, mainly in shades of red or yellow, flowering in late spring *23–45 × 30cm (9–18 × 12in)*.

Clay soils

The ideal garden soil is a medium loam: it retains moisture yet is well drained, with a fine, crumbly texture. However, many soils have a high clay content. Clay soils are usually very fertile and retain moisture. While this is an advantage, a very heavy wet soil tends to be difficult to work, and can often mean that plants become waterlogged. Always choose plants carefully to suit your soil type: there are many excellent plants, described below, that will thrive happily in clay.

Abelia × grandiflora
Rounded, vigorous, semi-evergreen shrub. Arching shoots with glossy, dark green leaves and an abundance of fragrant, tubular white flowers with pink tinges, lasting from mid summer to mid-autumn *3 × 3m (10 × 10ft)*.

Aruncus dioicus
Clump-forming perennial. Fern-like, toothed leaves and large feathery plumes of greenish white and creamy white flowers in early and mid summer. 'Kneiffii' is a dwarf form *1–2 × 1.2m (3–6½ × 4ft)*.

Aucuba japonica
Evergreen shrub. Glossy green leaves splashed or spotted yellow, insignificant flowers, but red fruits on female plants (plant a male variety for pollination) *2.4 × 2.4m (8 × 8ft)*.

Astilbe × arendsii hybrids
Clump-forming perennials. Fern-like foliage and spikes of plume-like flowerheads in summer in various colours, including: *A.* 'Fanal', in dark crimson; *A.* 'Federsee', in deep rose-pink; and *A.* 'Feuer', in salmon-pink *50–75cm × 45cm (20–30in × 18in)*, according to variety.

Berberis × stenophylla
Arching evergreen shrub. Spiny-tipped leaves and clusters of deep yellow flowers in late spring, followed by blue-black fruit *3 × 3m (10 × 10ft)*.

Cardamine pratensis 'Flore Pleno'
Clump-forming perennial. Leaves arranged in neat rosettes and loose clusters of double, lilac flowers in late spring *20 × 50cm (8 × 20in)*.

Chaenomeles japonica
Bushy deciduous shrub. Thorny with glossy leaves and clusters of orange

ABOVE: Rodgersia pinnata *is usually grown for the impact of its deeply veined leaves.*

RIGHT: *The panicles of* Astilbe 'Elizabeth Bloom' *appear in summer above bronze leaves.*

to red flowers in spring, followed by yellow or yellow-tinged fruit *1 × 2m (3 × 6½ft)*.

Crambe cordifolia
Clump-forming perennial. Large, dark green crinkled leaves and abundant tiny white, gypsophila-like flowers in late spring and mid summer *2.4 × 1.5m (8 × 5ft)*.

Digitalis grandiflora (syn. *D. orientalis*)
Clump-forming biennial or perennial. Tall spikes of pale yellow flowers in early and mid summer *100 × 45cm (39 × 18in)*.

Hemerocallis 'Burning Daylight'
Clump-forming perennial. Strap-shaped leaves, ending in a point at the tip, and bright orange, lily-like flowers in summer *1m × 75cm (3 × 2½ft)*.

Humulus lupulus 'Aureus'
Perennial climber. Bright, golden yellow lobed leaves and insignificant green flowers in summer, followed by decorative 'fruit' in autumn *6m (20ft)*.

Lathyrus grandiflorus
Perennial climber. Striking pink-purple and red, pea-like flowers from summer to early autumn *1.5m (5ft)*.

Leucanthemum × superbum hybrids (syn. *Chrysanthemum maximum*)
Clump-forming perennials. Chrysanthemum-like flowers in white with golden centres from early summer to early autumn. Various cultivars, which are better than the species: the dwarf 'Snow Lady'; 'Wirral Supreme', with large double flowers; and 'Phyllis Smith', with single flowers with twisted petals *45–90cm × 60cm (18–36in × 24in)*, according to variety.

Persicaria bistorta 'Superba' (syn. *Polygonum bistorta*)
Clump-forming, semi-evergreen perennial. Dense spires of soft pink flowers throughout summer *90 × 90cm (36 × 36in)*.

Phlox paniculata
Erect perennial. White, red, mauve,

ABOVE: Phormium tenax, *a clump-forming evergreen perennial, never fails to make a statement with its robust, architectural, sword-shaped leaves.*

pink flowers in summer *75 × 75cm (30 × 30in)*.

Phormium hybrids
Clump-forming evergreen perennial. Robust, upright, sword-shaped leaves in various colours *1–2.4 × 1m (3–8 × 3ft)*, according to variety.

Rodgersia pinnata 'Superba'
Clump-forming perennial. Deeply veined, crinkled leaves and plumes of yellowish white, pink or red star-shaped flowers which last from mid- and late summer *100 × 75cm (39 × 30in)*.

Tradescantia × andersoniana
Clump-forming perennial. Clusters of three-petalled, rich purple, blue or white flowers which last from early summer to early autumn and arching, strap-shaped leaves *50 × 50cm (20 × 20in)*.

BELOW: *In mid-summer large, feathery, creamy white plumes grace the tall, tough, sturdy stems of* Aruncus dioicus, *which is a clump-forming perennial.*

Pollution-tolerant plants

Town and city gardens, particularly those alongside a main road, are often exposed to very high levels of pollution. Many plants suffer extensively from the effects, while others thrive, despite the exhaust deposits collecting on their leaves. If you live in a busy, built-up area, select plants that are suitable for the conditions (see below), and reduce the impact by planting a dense hedge of pollution-tolerant plants around the edge of the garden.

Amelanchier canadensis
Erect deciduous shrub. Orange-red foliage in autumn and star-shaped white flowers in spring, sometimes followed by blue-black fruit *6 × 3m (20 × 10ft)*.

Aucuba japonica
Rounded evergreen shrub. Glossy, leathery oval leaves, often toothed, and small red-purple flowers in mid spring *2.4 × 2.4m (8 × 8ft)*.

Berberis
Evergreen or deciduous shrubs. Attractive leaves, some holly-like and many with good autumn colour, yellow to dark orange flowers, and colourful fruit. Wide range of sizes from dwarf or mound-forming (*B. thunbergii* 'Bagatelle') to vigorous and upright (*B.* 'Goldilocks'); some are useful for hedging (*B. thunbergii*) *50cm–4m × 45cm–4m (20in–13ft × 18in–13ft)*, according to species of variety.

Buddleia davidii
Arching deciduous shrub. Dense trusses of fragrant lilac to purple flowers from summer to autumn *3 × 5m (10 × 16½ft)*.

Ceratostigma willmottianum
Spreading deciduous shrub. Dark green, purple-edged leaves that turn red in autumn, and a display of blue flowers with red-purple tubes from late summer to autumn *1 × 1.5m (3 × 5ft)*.

Chaenomeles hybrids
Deciduous shrubs. Spiny with cup-shaped flowers in pink, red, orange or white in early spring to summer, followed by edible fruit. Some suitable for ground cover or low hedging (*C. japonica*), others for a border (*C. speciosa* and *C. × superba* varieties) *1–3m × 2–5m (3–10ft × 6½–16½ft)*, according to species or variety.

ABOVE LEFT: *Elaeagnus × ebbingei 'Gilt Edge' makes a good screen.*

ABOVE: *Berberis have spectacular flower displays in spring, and deciduous kinds have tinted foliage in autumn.*

Cotoneaster frigidus
Upright then spreading deciduous tree or large shrub. White, saucer-shaped flowers in summer, followed by orange-red fruit *5 × 5m (15 × 15ft)*.

Elaeagnus × ebbingei
Rounded evergreen shrub. Attractive glossy leaves, silvery beneath, and creamy, silvery white flowers in autumn *4 × 4m (13 × 13ft)*.

Elaegnus pungens
Bushy evergreen shrub. Glossy, often wavy-edged leaves and pendent, silvery white flowers in autumn, followed by brown-red fruit *4 × 5m (13 × 16½ft)*.

Border and rock plants

Achillea filipendulina (bees, butterflies)
Alyssum saxatile (butterflies)
Armeria maritima (bees, butterflies)
Aster novi-beglii (bees, butterflies)
Erigeron (bees, butterflies)
Nepeta (bees, butterflies)
Scabiosa caucasica (bees, butterflies)
Sedum spectabile (bees, butterflies)
Solidago (birds, bees, butterflies)
Thymus (bees, butterflies)

Annuals and biennials

Centaurea cyanus (bees, butterflies)
Dipsacus spp. (birds)
Helianthus annus (birds)
Hesperis matronalis (bees)
Limnanthes douglasii (bees)
Lunaria annua (birds)
Scabiosa annual (bees, butterflies)

LEFT: Sedum *'Autumn Joy'*

BELOW: Solidago.

ABOVE: Alyssum saxatile.

OTHER WAYS TO ATTRACT WILDLIFE

A thick hedge attracts far more wildlife than a fence or wall. A prickly evergreen hedge like holly will provide good nest and roost sites for many birds.

An old log pile provides refuge for many beneficial insects and can make a nest site for small mammals.

The Kitchen Garden

Ambitious kitchen gardens are seldom achievable in a small space. Vegetables that are hungry for space such as potatoes and cabbages may lose out to flowers. But if you are content with smaller vegetables such as lettuces, carrots, beetroot, and dwarf beans, and can relegate tall climbing beans and expansive plants like globe artichokes to the mixed or herbaceous border, it is quite practical to grow a wide range of vegetables even where space is quite restricted.

Grow a whole range of vegetables, from lettuces to peas, in containers like windowboxes

ABOVE: *Raspberries are not an ideal crop for a small garden but they can be trained so that they don't take up too much space.*

TOP: *Fruit-growing is possible even on a roof or balcony garden . . . with a little imagination.*

OPPOSITE: *This picture shows an interesting way of providing supports for tall vegetables in a small kitchen garden.*

LEFT: *One of the upright-growing apple trees ideal for a small garden or limited space. This variety is 'Walz', planted in a bed of 'Surrey' ground cover roses.*

and growing bags. Even potatoes can be harvested from pots and growing bags and tomatoes of all types have been grown with great success in growing bags. This kind of small-scale vegetable gardening is demanding, and the yields always very modest for the effort involved, but if the idea of harvesting your own fresh vegetables just before you pop them into the pot appeals, you may find it worth the effort. It can certainly be fun.

If you have a reasonably sized garden – large enough to divide off a section for a kitchen garden – growing them in the ground is the most practical way to produce your vegetables, and much of the fruit.

Fruit trees and bushes are often ornamental and can be easily integrated into the flower garden. Trained fruit trees like espalier and fan apples look attractive even with bare branches in winter.

Herbs are much more easily accommodated than vegetables. Many are highly ornamental and lots of them make good container plants. Others look perfectly in place in a border. If you want to make a real feature of your herbs, make a herb garden a key part of your garden design.

Ornamental herbs

Formal herb gardens look impressive, but can be difficult to accommodate in a small space. However, as the illustrations below show, there are alternatives.

Bear in mind that though herb gardens are packed with interest in summer, in winter you will be left with just a few evergreen shrubs and a handful of herbs that retain their foliage and are tough enough to survive unprotected. Alternatively, incorporate your herbs in an overall garden design that carries interest through all the seasons. Here are some other ways to incorporate herbs in a small garden.

A collection in a container
A herb pot can hold half a dozen or more different herbs. Do not start to harvest until plants are growing strongly, then keep harvesting little and often to produce compact yet well-clothed plants.

Shrubby plants like bay and rosemary can be grown in tubs to decorate the patio or to display by the front or back door.

Windowbox herbs
Herbs can be grown in windowboxes and troughs provided you choose compact plants such as thymes and marjorams. Ornamental, variegated mints also look good.

Growing bags
Growing bags are not elegant, but they are useful for rampant plants like mints, which would otherwise make a take-over bid for the border.

In among the flowers
Many herbs are so decorative that they don't look amiss in beds and borders, and indeed some are planted more for their ornamental than culinary uses.

Among the herbs that look good with other border plants are chives, fennel, marjoram, and lemon balm.

ABOVE: *Have fun with your small herbs. They can be arranged informally in pots, or grouped together as in the small wheelbarrow.*

RIGHT: *An attractive herb collection can be grown in a small raised bed, but bear in mind that many of these plants will grow much larger.*

Ornamental potagers

The term potager comes from jardin potager, simply being French for kitchen garden. But the term has come to refer primarily to a kitchen garden – usually with both fruit and vegetables – laid out ornamentally, perhaps with beds edged with low hedges like a parterre. Treated like this, your kitchen garden can become a prominent design element.

Growing bags

Growing bags are excellent for vegetables if all you have is a balcony or patio on which to grow them. It is quite feasible to grow lettuces, spinach, radishes, cucumbers, tomatoes, turnips, even self-blanching celery and potatoes, in growing bags.

Clearly, you won't keep the family fed with potatoes from a couple of growing bags, and the economics don't make much sense. But it is

ABOVE: *These are 'Totem' tomatoes growing in a 25cm (10in) pot.*
BELOW: *You can even grow tomatoes in a hanging basket.*

worth planting an early variety (you can move the bag into a protected area if frost threatens) so that you can enjoy those new potatoes straight from the garden.

Troughs, tubs and pots

Tomatoes are one of the most successful crops for a growing bag, and, provided you choose a suitable compact variety, they are equally successful in pots.

Courgettes (zucchini) and cucumbers are also a practical choice for a tub or large pot. Potatoes can be grown in a pot for a bit of fun, but you might be better planting an aubergine (eggplant) or pepper in it.

Windowboxes and hanging baskets

The only vegetable likely to do well in a hanging basket is the tomato, but you must choose a trailing or drooping variety, and control both watering and feeding.

Windowboxes offer more scope and, apart from tomatoes (use dwarf or trailing varieties), stump-rooted carrots, radishes, onions and lettuces are among the crops that do well.

Rather than grow a hearting lettuce, which leaves a gap as the whole head is harvested at once, try a non-hearting 'cut-and-come-again' variety that you can harvest in stages.

Flowers and vegetables

If you simply don't have the space to devote part of your garden to vegetables and herbs alone, consider integrating them with the existing ornamentals. Many vegetables are pretty in their own right – with striking foliage and flowers – and when grown in beds and borders, and intermixed with other decorative plants, they can work surprisingly well.

One of the enormous advantages of growing vegetables with flowers is that the diversity of plants helps to deter pests and diseases. Mixed planting provides a naturally balanced environment, where the flowers attract insects and other wildlife that feed on pests that feed on vegetables. Sowing marigolds among tomato plants, for example, will keep the tomatoes relatively free from attack by aphids, because the marigolds attract hover-flies, and their larvae like nothing better than an aphid feast.

Among the flowers
It is quite possible to incorporate vegetables as part of a formal bedding scheme. Red or purple rhubarb chard leaves, for example, contrast well with grey-foliaged bedding plants; carrot foliage looks attractive as a foil for bright summer bedding plants; and even one of the more decorative kinds of red-leaved lettuce will make a pretty edging for a summer bedding scheme. Unfortunately, the problem comes at harvest time, when gaps soon become rather conspicuous.

Vegetables are more acceptable as gap fillers in a herbaceous or mixed border. They fill the space admirably, and after harvesting the border is left no less attractive than it was originally. If you choose crops such as spinach or 'cut-and-come again' (oak leaf) lettuce, you can harvest the leaves without destroying the whole

LEFT: *Edging a vegetable plot with colourful flowers is the best solution if you want vegetables and ornamentals.*

ABOVE: *Rosemary (*Rosmarinus officinalis*) is a herb that tastes as good as it looks.*

ABOVE: *When young, purple sage (*Salvia officinalis *'Purpurascens') has tinged foliage.*

ABOVE: *Mint (*Mentha*) is highly invasive and should be planted in pots in the ground.*

plant. Other suitable candidates here are radishes, beetroot, asparagus peas, carrots, and leaf beet; but much depends on the size of your space and your imagination.

In a traditional cottage garden, where flowers rub shoulders with fruit, vegetables and herbs, the plants often merge into one another but the result can appear rather chaotic. If the rest of the garden is formal in style, dedicate just one area to mixed planting and make it a feature, separated with a hedge or screen.

Planting in blocks

Instead of having single vegetable plants dotted here and there among the flowers, try growing them in blocks or patches. The effect can be just as decorative, and the crops will certainly be easier to harvest, after which the space can easily be replanted. Plant the areas that had vegetables in summer with winter-flowering bulbs and spring bedding. That way, you will gain more ornamental value without sacrificing much in terms of crop.

With such small patches of ground, it takes no time at all to sow a batch of seed, tend delicate young

plants, or keep weeds under control. Using this method, you may grow the same quantity of vegetables as in a conventional plot but the task will seem far less daunting.

Climbing vegetables

Most climbing vegetables are decorative in themselves, and you can treat them in much the same way as you would any ornamental annual climbers. Make a feature of ordinary or asparagus peas by

ABOVE: *Brushing past low-growing thymes (*Thymus*), such as this one with its delicate pink flowers, will release a pungent scent.*

growing them against a free-standing trellis or a wall of canes and netting within the flower border. Train trailing forms of courgette (zucchini) over an archway or pergola. Or grow ridge cucumbers and scarlet runner beans on wigwams (tepees) of canes at the back of a border or along a series of rustic poles lining the path.

Getting Started

To enjoy your container garden from its inception, begin by
choosing the best-shaped container for each planting and one
that will show off the plants to their full advantage. Plants
suitable for container gardening can be planted in the right
compost (soil mix), in standing pots or in baskets or half-pots
fixed to a wall as hanging gardens. Then, with regular
feeding and watering (keeping a watchful eye open for
signs of pests and diseases) you should have a success on
your hands.

ABOVE: *The soft petals and subtle*
colour gradations of the violas make
them the perfect match for the pearly
interiors of the shells.

OPPOSITE: *Even garden tools and*
empty containers can make decorative
ornaments to complement a
beautifully arranged window box.

The best plants for containers

Annuals and Biennials

Whether you raise them yourself from seed in the greenhouse or on the kitchen window-sill, or buy them in strips from the garden centre for an instant effect, fast-growing annuals and biennials will quickly and cheaply fill baskets and boxes and flower prolifically all summer to produce eye-catching effects. Choose compact varieties that will not need support. Trailing annuals such as lobelia, nasturtiums and dwarf sweet peas are all invaluable for hanging baskets. Some perennial species, including petunias, pelargoniums and busy Lizzies (impatiens), are normally grown as annuals.

Tender Perennials

Beautiful tender and half-hardy plants such as osteospermums, verbenas, pelargoniums, petunias and fuchsias are ideal for containers, where their showy flowers can be fully appreciated. Raise new plants from cuttings for next season. If you buy young, tender plants from the garden centre in the spring, don't be tempted to put newly planted boxes or baskets outside until all danger of frost is past.

ABOVE: *Trailing nasturtiums make a glorious display, providing colour from early summer.*

LEFT: *Petunias and pelargoniums are tender perennials, which are often grown as annuals.*

BELOW: *Containers of spring bulbs such as these yellow tulips cannot fail to delight.*

Evergreen Perennials

Evergreen non-woody perennials such as ajugas, bergenias and *Carex oshimensis* 'Evergold' are always useful for providing colour and foliage in the winter, but look best as part of a mixed planting.

For single plantings, try *Agapanthus africanus* or *A. orientalis* with their blue flowers on tall stems. For a more architectural shape, consider one of the many different eryngiums (sea holly). *E. agavifolium* is particularly attractive, and has greenish-white flowers in late summer.

Border Perennials

Few people bother to grow perennials in containers, but if you have a paved garden, or would like to introduce them to the patio, don't be afraid to exper-iment. Dicentras, agapanthus, and many ornamental grasses are among the plants that you might want to try, but there are very many more that you should be able to succeed with – and they will cost you nothing if you divide a plant already in the border.

Bulbs

Bulbs, particularly the spring varieties make ideal container plants. Bulbs should be planted at twice the depth of their own length. They can be packed in as tight as you like, and even in layers, so that you get a repeat-showing after the first display. Note that when planting lilies (the white, scented, fail-safe *Lilium regale* is a fine choice if you have never tried them before), they need excellent drainage, so put in an extra layer of grit at the bottom. And to prevent spearing the bulb later on with a plant support, insert this in the compost at the same time.

Shrubs for Tubs

Camellias are perfect shrubs for tubs, combining attractive, glossy evergreen foliage with beautiful spring flowers. *Camellia* x *williamsii* and *C. japonica* hybrids are a good choice. Many rhododendrons and azaleas are also a practical proposition, and if you have a chalky (alkaline) soil this is the best way to grow these plants – provided you fill the container with an ericaceous compost (soil mix).

Many hebes make good container plants (but not for very cold or exposed areas), and there are many attractively variegated varieties. The yellow-leaved *Choisya ternata* 'Sundance' and variegated yuccas such as *Yucca filamentosa* 'Variegata' and *Y. gloriosa* 'Variegata' are also striking shrubs for containers.

For some winter interest, try *Viburnum tinus*.

Topiary for Pots

Topiarized box is ideal for a pot. However, it is relatively slow growing at about 30cm (12in) a year. It may be best to buy a mature, ready-shaped plant, although you miss the fun of doing the pruning.

ABOVE: *If your garden cannot support lime-hating rhododendrons, do not despair. They can easily be grown in pots, in ericaceous compost (soil mix), giving colour from autumn, through winter, to summer.*

LEFT: *Pots on plinths and fruit trees in tubs create a marvellous architectural effect, with plenty of striking verticals.*

Trees for Tubs

Trees are unlikely candidates for containers, particularly for small gardens. Fortunately, the restricted root-run usually keeps them compact and they never reach the proportions of trees planted in the ground. Even in a small garden, some height is useful.

Choose trees that are naturally small if possible. Laburnums, crab apples (and some of the upright-growing and compact eating apples on dwarfing rootstocks), *Prunus* 'Amanogawa' (a flowering cherry with narrow, upright growth), and even trees as potentially large as *Acer platanoides* 'Drummondii' (a variegated maple) will be happy in a large pot or tub for a number of years. Small weeping trees also look good. Try *Salix caprea pendula* or *Cotoneaster* 'Hybridus Pendulus' (which has cascades of red berries in autumn). Even the pretty dome-shaped, grey-leaved *Pyrus salicifolia* 'Pendula' is a possibility.

These must have a heavy pot with a minimum inside diameter of 38cm (15in), and a loam-based compost (soil mix). Even then they are liable to blow over in very strong winds unless you pack some other hefty pots around them during stormy weather.

Providing year-round colour

Containers are traditionally used for creating extra, lavish colourful effects in summer. With a little thought and careful planning you can enjoy delightful containers all year round.

First Signs of Spring

Early spring bulbs burst into life as soon as winter loosens its grip. Even on chilly, rainy days, pots planted with small bulbs – snowdrops, crocuses, scillas and *Iris reticulata* – will provide splashes of clear colour on the patio or window-sills, and can be briefly brought indoors, if you like, for an early taste of spring. Primulas and polyanthus look great in containers, too. If you grow lily-of-the-valley in the garden, pot up a few roots and bring them inside: they'll come into bloom weeks early.

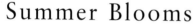

ABOVE AND LEFT:
Plants might not flourish in the garden border all year round, but you can still have some delightful plants every day of the year. Here, small pots of lily-of-the-valley, dwarf irises, crocuses and primroses brighten up a warm day in early spring.

Summer Blooms

Summer is, of course, the highlight of the container gardener's year, giving the opportunity for lovely creative plantings. Deciding which plants to use is an enjoyable task.

RIGHT: *For a really eye-catching container, be different. A large potted mix, featuring summer bedding plants topped by a lanky white fuchsia, is encircled by a rustic woven sheep feeder. The effect is heightened by tufts of grass packed into the gaps.*

FAR RIGHT: *A flamboyant show of billowing annuals.*

OPPOSITE: *An orange-yellow poppy and cream-coloured violas look stunning planted in beige pots, set against the warm ochre shades of a brick wall.*

ABOVE: *This pot has been painted in stripes to link the green background and pink blooms of a wonderful hebe.*

Colour-splash plantings

Just as you can decorate the inside of your home with colourful flower arrangements, so you can do the same outside. Use pots of flowering plants to provide a colourful splash in a prominent part of the garden or to decorate the outdoor living area when entertaining. Create an immediate colour impact by choosing a colour theme and teaming containers and plants in toning shades. Try painting some terracotta pots specially to match your favourite flowers. You could also make a tablescape for a special occasion, using a variety of containers and seasonal flowering plants in hot clashing colours or in cool shades of blue, purple and white.

ABOVE: *Simple and magical, it is as though the rich colouring of the tulips has leaked out of the petals and dripped down the side of the pots.*

ABOVE: *Even a couple of ordinary terracotta garden pots hanging on the wall make interesting decorative detail, especially when they are both planted with a froth of white blooms.*

LEFT: *This vivid arrangement of winter-flowering pansies in a trug can be moved around to provide colour wherever it is needed.*

ABOVE: *Bright, bold, hothouse colours are very effective in groups.*
Try to find equally brightly coloured planters and containers.

Creating cameo gardens

If you are lucky enough to have a spare part of the garden where nothing is going on, liven it up by introducing a set theme. It can be witty and original, or have a theme to merge with the rest of the garden. Or it could even be a special private area packed with all your favourite pots.

Cameo gardens can provide a surprise in a small corner, embellish an under-used area or even provide a miniature project for children, who love to have a space of their own. The idea is to find a theme – herbs, perhaps, or pansies, miniature vegetables or lavender – then make up a 'sampler', providing a different container for each variety. Alternatively, you can make the containers the theme, choosing watering-cans, culinary pots, pans and colanders, enamelware or terracotta in different shapes and sizes. Another idea is to design a miniature formal garden, perhaps taking inspiration from the classic Italian style. Choose a piece of small statuary as a focal point, then clip some young box plants into a miniature hedge surround and fill in with dwarf lavender.

LEFT: *For a seaside-type garden, use a stone-coloured pot and grey-leaved plants to blend in with the sandy background.*

Pots for Privacy

To be able to relax totally in the garden, you need to satisfy two basic requirements: privacy and shelter. Without the benefit of enclosed spaces, especially in built-up areas, these considerations can be problematic. However, there are ways of achieving them. Trellis can be fixed on top of walls and fences to create extra height. You can then grow decorative climbers to provide a wonderful natural wallpaper. And within this enclosure you can create a special atmosphere with the use of gorgeous pots. In fact, pots score over plants in beds because they can be swapped round with other containers in the rest of the garden, giving a constant change of scenery.

One way of conveying privacy is by furnishing this area like a real room. A row of shelves for a collection of, say, pelargoniums, pouring out rich red and magenta flowers and subtler hues. Verbenas make an excellent alternative, and can either be left to tumble, or trained up miniature wigwams (teepees) of green sticks to provide a side-show in blues, mauves and purples, interspersed with white. Violas are equally small-scale and domestic, with the added advantage that, being placed at eye level, their amazingly exquisite, detailed patterning can be fully appreciated. But perhaps the best container plants for outdoor shelving, or even an old, brightly painted open kitchen display unit, are auricula primulas.

Auriculas impart a strong Victorian feel (although they were actually introduced in the late 16th century) with their ornate faces, which are so exquisite that they used to be displayed inside an empty picture frame. One by itself is always an eye-catcher, leaving the viewer demanding more. Visit a specialist nursery to see a wide range.

Scented Pots

An enclosed area with no wind is the perfect place to grow scented pot plants where the perfume can hang in the air. You can have anything from marzipan to the smell of melting, rich brown chocolate. Just place the pots around a chair, sit back and relax.

Daphne odora 'Aureomarginata' makes a perfect shrub for a tub. It grows quite slowly to about 1.5m (5ft), and has purplish flowers, and the most ravishing scent imaginable. Feed well, place in the sun, and add plenty of grit to the soil for quick drainage.

Jasminum officinale is a fast, vigorous climber; it will quickly race up the side of a house or, with a restricted root run, can be trained round a large frame. Give it a hot sunny spot, water well, and inhale. Lilies have equally strong scents. The range is huge, running from the highly popular and reliable *Lilium regale* to the various, multi-coloured hybrids like 'Black Dragon' and 'Green Dragon', to the stunning strain called Imperial Crimson, with white flowers speckled red. Good drainage is the secret of success.

For a talking point, choose the unusual but wonderful *Cosmos atrosanguineus* which has dark maroon flowers and a whiff of chocolate on hot, sunny days. For marzipan, try an old-fashioned heliotrope like 'Princess Marina'. And for an unusual small black flower and the scent of summer fruits, plant up *Salvia discolor*.

RIGHT: *Thyme-filled gardens have a distinguished history, and have been popular since the medieval period. The trick is to choose a selection, with round and needle-like leaves, to create a rich tapestry in shades of green, gold and silver.*

Novel Themes

Edible gardens are always popular, and besides growing potted fruit trees and strawberries, it is worth experimenting with different kinds of salad. Lettuces now come in a wide range of shapes and colours and the more ornamental forms of herbs like basil and sage are just as delicious as the green varieties.

You can also grow a range of potted plants with different textured foliage. Smooth and svelte, sharp and pointed, rubbery and mounded, are all available. When next visiting a garden centre, do not just go in with your eyes open but with a stroking, extended hand. Plants appeal to more senses than one.

ABOVE: *A marvellous concoction made from the simplest of easily gathered materials. A scattering of wet beach pebbles frames a circular pattern, backed up by a group of small pots and chimney pots, planted with a wide selection of succulents.*

TOP: *Serried ranks of watering-cans in the soft greys of weathered, galvanized metal make a beautiful feature in themselves. Planted up with hostas and violas, they become a highly original cameo garden.*

ABOVE: *This terracotta garden is focused around tall, long-tom pots planted with hostas, ivies and clematis let loose so that it behaves like a trailer, rather than a climber. Old drain covers and edging tiles add character.*

LEFT: *Potted plants always give plenty of impact when arranged in groups and one way to display them is on old baker's shelves in rows and rows of pots.*

RIGHT: *Themed gardens do not come much better than this. A sensational group of battered, wizened old boots double up as containers. The sumptuous profusion of pelargoniums in full blast obviously couldn't be happier.*

Living table decorations

Outdoor table decorations are easy to put together and are at their most successful when they complement their surroundings. Simply gather together some of the smaller pots from around the garden, you may plunder the garden for a few cut flowers or foliage to add, or even add fruit and vegetables to complete the effect. The concentration in one place of what grows in naturally looser arrangements throughout the garden focuses the overall look.

BELOW: *Spring narcissi are perfectly in scale for a table setting. And with so many varieties having strong scents, there's nowhere better to appreciate them while relaxing over a long cold drink.*

Containers as Screens, and with Arbours and Arches

Where you have a garden eyesore, such as a crumbling outhouse or drainage pipe, use ingenuity and imagination to hide it. You do not need to go overboard. A large pot containing a prolific marguerite (argyranthemum) will produce hundreds of daisy-like blooms all summer. You could even grow this plant as a standard, with a mop-head of growth on a 90cm (3ft) high single stem. A planted container, whether hanging or on the ground, is a lovely finishing touch to a garden arch or arbour.

TOP: *This arbour would look very bare without its glorious hanging basket of petunias.*

ABOVE: *A pair of formal containers planted with fuchsia standards, complement this garden archway perfectly.*

LEFT: *A colourful windowbox is used here to mark the edge of a border.*

Types of Container

One of the challenges of container gardening is finding the right container for the right setting. You can now quite readily buy a whole range of lovely containers, for example, waist-high, Italian olive oil jars make a terrific focal point – big and bold and stylish. At the other end of the scale, you can be as imaginative as you like. You could use a Wellington boot or an old shoe for an engaging, quirky touch. In between, of course, the choice is huge: rustic terracotta, voguish metal or brightly painted cans, Mediterranean style.

It is important to consider the final setting when you are buying a container. A rustic tub may look charming under the window of a thatched cottage, but inappropriate outside a formal town house. Bear proportions in mind and, for example, choose a windowbox that exactly fits the sill. It is also worth noting that the weight of a container, when filled with compost (soil mix) and freshly watered, will be considerably greater than when empty. Think twice before packing your roof terrace or balcony with heavy pots: the structure may not be able to cope. And never leave a container on a window-sill from where it could fall down into the street.

Stone troughs

NOT SO READILY AVAILABLE BUT DEFINITELY WORTH LOOKING AT.

Advantages – durable and attractive.

Disadvantages – very heavy and expensive.

Pots and barrels

VERSATILE AND PRACTICAL.

Advantages – maintenance-free and versatile.

Disadvantages – heavy to move.

Wooden windowboxes

GIVE A WOODEN CONTAINER AN ORIGINAL LOOK WITH YOUR OWN COLOUR SCHEME.

Advantages – you can change the look to suit any new planting scheme.

Disadvantages – the boxes require occasional maintenance.

Terracotta windowboxes

AVAILABLE IN A WIDE RANGE OF SIZES AND STYLES.

Advantages – look good and appear even better with age.

Disadvantages – heavy, and may be damaged by frost.

Galvanized tin

TIN HAS MOVED FROM THE UTILITARI-
AN TO THE FASHIONABLE.

Advantages – an interesting variation from the usual materials.

Disadvantages – drainage holes
required.

Lightweight fibre windowboxes

PLAIN AND PRACTICAL.

Advantages – look rustic, and have a rich
brown colour.

Disadvantages – short life-span.

Baskets

CAN BE USED AS WINDOWBOXES
PROVIDED THEY ARE GENEROUSLY
LINED WITH MOSS BEFORE PLANTING.

Advantages – lightweight and
attractive.

Disadvantages – plant pots must
be removed for watering, or the
base of the basket will be soaked
and rot.

Types of hanging baskets

Before you choose the plants and plan how to
arrange them, decide first what style of hanging
basket you are going to display them in. Garden
centres stock a huge variety, which are all easy
to work with and hang. Hanging baskets are
made from plastic-coated wire, wrought-iron and
galvanized wire.

Hanging baskets

VARIED AND PRACTICAL.

Advantages – look lovely planted.

Disadvantages – need to be
lined before use.

Novelty containers

HUGELY UNDERRATED. USE ANYTHING FROM
WATERING-CANS OR TYRES TO SHOES.

Advantages – witty and fun.

Disadvantages – possible short life-span.

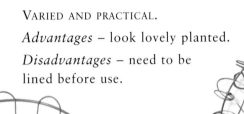

Choosing composts (soil mixes)

Composts (soil mixes) come in various formulations to suit different plant requirements. A standard potting compost is usually peat-based and is suitable for all purposes. Peat and peat substitutes are relatively light in weight and therefore the best choice for hanging baskets. Regular watering is vital when using peat-based composts, as it is very difficult to moisten them again if they have been allowed to dry out completely. Different composts can be mixed together for specific plant needs.

Standard compost (soil mix)

The majority of composts available at garden centres are peat-based with added fertilizers.

Container compost (soil mix)

A peat-based compost with moisture-retaining granules and added fertilizer, specially formulated for windowboxes and containers.

Ericaceous compost (soil mix)

A peat-based compost with no added lime, essential for rhododendrons, camellias and heathers in containers.

Peat-free compost (soil mix)

Manufacturers now offer a range of composts using materials from renewable resources such as coir fibre. They are used in the same way as peat-based composts.

Loam-based compost (soil mix)

Uses sterilized loam as the main ingredient, with fertilizers to supplement the nutrients in the loam. Although much heavier than peat-based compost, it can be lightened by mixing with peat-free compost. Ideal for long-term planting as it retains nutrients well.

THE ESSENTIAL FERTILIZER ELEMENTS

All plant fertilizers contain three key elements, nitrogen (N), phosphorous (P), and potassium/potash (K), with extra trace elements. These three promote, respectively, foliage growth, flower development, and fruit ripening and root development.

When buying a packet of fertilizer you can easily check the balance of the ingredients. It is printed as an "NPK" ratio, for instance 12:5:12. But don't be fooled into thinking that a reading of 24:10:24 is stronger, giving twice the value. It won't, of course, as the ratio is the same. A fertilizer with a ratio of 10:5:10 provides a sound, balanced diet. (You can purchase meters from garden centres that give a guide to the nutrient levels in the soil but they are not, to date, particularly accurate.)

Besides feeding, you can also trick some plants into a prolific display of flowering. Plants packed into small containers, with restricted (but not crippling) root space, feel that they are in danger of dying. Their immediate response is to do what all flowering plants are programmed to do – flower and set seed to continue the species.

Feeding container plants

It is not generally understood that most potting composts (soil mixes) contain sufficient food for only six weeks of plant growth. After that, the plants will slowly starve unless more food is introduced. There are several products available, all of which are easy to use. Many of the projects in this book use slow-release plant food granules because they are the easiest and most reliable way of ensuring your plants receive sufficient food during the growing season. For these granules to be effective the compost needs to remain damp or the nutrients cannot be released.

Slow-release Plant Food Granules

These will keep your container plants in prime condition and are very easy to use. One application lasts six months, whereas most other plant foods need to be applied fortnightly. Follow the manufacturer's recommended dose carefully; additional fertilizer will simply leach away.

BELOW: *A variety of plant foods (clockwise from top left): liquid foliar feed, two types of pelleted slow-release plant food granules, a general fertilizer and loose slow-release plant food granules.*

TOP: *Slow-release plant food granules can be added to the compost (soil mix) in the recommended quantity before filling the container and planting it.*

ABOVE: *When adding fertilizer granules to the soil, sprinkle them on to the surface of the compost (soil mix) and rake into the top layer. Pelleted granules should be pushed approximately 2cm (³⁄4in) below the surface.*

Planting pots and planters

Planting up a container of any size could not be easier, as long as you follow a few basic rules. First, terracotta pots need a layer of material at the bottom to help the water drain away quickly. Plastic pots usually have sufficient drainage holes. Second, always plant into the appropriate size pot; that is, slightly larger than the root-ball. Putting a small plant into a large pot is counter productive. The plant will put on good root growth at the expense of flowers and foliage. Since the hungry root system will drink up water rapidly in summer, check regularly that the soil is not too dry.

ABOVE: *Beautiful, elegant urns do not always need the finest flowering plants. As these twin pots show, even a modest planting works well. Indeed, it is often preferable because it does not detract from the gorgeous containers.*

Maintaining Plants

Large plants can grow in surprisingly small containers. They will not grow to the same height as if they were given a free root run, but should be impressive nonetheless. If possible, remove the top layer of soil every year, and replace it with fresh compost (soil mix). There comes a time, however, when most plants finally outgrow their containers. What then? You can replace the mature plant with a cutting and start again. Alternatively, stick instead to plants that are slow-growing, or which will not rapidly fill their pots with roots. Or root prune.

Root pruning is a remarkably easy technique, which involves removing the plant from the pot in spring, when it is beginning to put on good growth. Either slice away the exterior of the root-ball quite boldly, or snip at it with secateurs. Then replace in the existing pot, filling the gap with fresh compost.

Overwintering

Remember that while tender plants may just survive winter outside in your area, with their roots protected deep below ground, those in pots are much less likely to survive. The roots will be just the thickness of the pot away from encircling snow or icy winds. Bring these plants indoors or, if there's no room, take cuttings before the end of the season.

Planting in Terracotta

Terracotta containers are always popular, but need some preparation before planting.

1 With terracotta it is essential to provide some form of drainage material in the base of the container. When planting in large pots or boxes, recycle broken-up polystyrene (plastic foam) plant trays as drainage material. Lumps of polystyrene are excellent for this use and as they retain warmth they are of additional benefit to the plant.

2 In smaller pots the drainage material can be broken pieces of pot, known as crocks, or gravel.

Planting in Plastic

When buying plastic pots or boxes, check that the drainage holes are open. Some manufacturers mark the holes but leave it to the purchaser to punch or drill them out as required.

Plant Supports

Climbing plants in containers will need support. This can be provided by one or more canes which are pushed into the pot, a free-standing plant frame or a trellis fastened to a wall behind the container.

Planting in Wicker Baskets

If you wish to use a more unconventional container as a windowbox you may need to seal it with a sheet of plastic to prevent leakage.

1 Line the basket with a generous layer of moss which will prevent the compost (soil mix) leaking away.

2 Fill the basket with compost (soil mix), and mix in plant food granules or any organic alternative.

Saucers and Feet

Saucers are available for plastic and clay pots. They act as water reservoirs for the plants, and are used under houseplants to protect the surface they are standing on. Clay saucers must be fully glazed if they are used indoors or they will leave marks. Clay feet are available for terracotta pots. They will prevent the pot becoming waterlogged, but this also means that in a sunny position the pot will dry out very quickly and may need extra watering.

Plastic plant saucers can be used to line and protect containers which are not waterproof, such as this wooden apple-basket.

Planting hanging baskets

When you want colour high up or relating closely to the building, the easiest way is to create a hanging garden, either in baskets or in wall-mounted containers. A purpose-made hanging basket is designed so that as the flowers grow, they cascade through the side and spill over the edge in a joyous show of colour, covering the whole basket. An alternative is to make the basket or container part of the display. Ordinary shopping baskets, buckets, agricultural containers, even kitchen equipment such as colanders, pots and pans, can be used.

Planting and Positioning Hanging Baskets

One hanging basket, alone on a wall, can look rather insignificant. Far better to plant up baskets in pairs, either with similar plants to create an echoing effect, or with clashing, contrasting colours. For a really stunning effect, entirely cover a wall with baskets, but remember that they are very demanding, and will need prolific watering in a dry mid-summer.

If the container is large and in danger of getting too heavy for its support, one trick is to put a layer of broken-up expanded polystyrene (plastic foam), from plant trays or electrical goods packaging, in the bottom of the container. This is lighter than the equivalent amount of compost (soil mix) and provides good drainage. Containers should have drainage holes, and baskets will need lining to stop the soil from being washed out while

you are watering. Liners can be home-made from pieces of plastic sheet cut to size, with a layer of moss tucked between the basket and plastic for a more decorative look. Alternatively, you can use a proprietary liner, made from paper pulp, to fit purpose-made hanging baskets, or coconut matting – which comes in a variety of shapes and sizes to adapt to all kinds of baskets.

Whichever type of container you choose, it needs to be filled with a good compost, and adding fertilizer granules and water-retaining gel can also help promote lush results and make care and maintenance a little easier.

RIGHT: *Hanging baskets filled with pansies create a lovely focal point of gentle colour.*

Tin can plant nursery

Seedlings can be decorative in themselves, so prick them out from their seed trays into a collection of shiny aluminum cans mounted on to a plaque. They can grow there until they are ready to be planted out. The plaque itself looks wonderful made from ordinary aluminum cans, but if you want to add a bit more colour, scour the shelves of delicatessens for some unusual printed cans and enjoy some culinary treats at the same time.

MATERIALS

Piece of board, about
  60 x 30cm (24 x 12in)
Undercoat
Coloured gloss paint
Decorating brush
Can opener
Variety of empty
  aluminium cans with
  the labels removed

Metal snippers
Pliers
Nail
Hammer
Tin tacks

1 Apply an undercoat followed by a coat of gloss paint to the board, allowing each coat to dry completely.

2 Use the can opener to remove the top of each can if this has not already been done. Wash out the cans thoroughly.

3 Using metal snippers, cut down the side of each can and cut off half of the bottom.

4 Open out the sides with pliers and snip a V-shape into each one. Pierce the bottom of each can, using a nail and hammer.

5 Try out the arrangement of the cans on the board. Then, using one tin tack at each side point of the cans, nail into position.

Mexican painted pots

A series of traditional folk-art motifs painted over stripes of vibrant colours gives simple pots a rich Mexican look. Enhance the effect by allowing some of the untreated terracotta colour show through, especially if you use pots with a fluted top like this one. Planted up with pelargoniums in hot summer colours, and stacked together, they make a lively garden feature.

MATERIALS

Terracotta pot with fluted-top
Masking tape
White undercoat
Small decorating brush
Artist's gouache paints
Fine and medium artist's brushes
Polyurethane matt varnish

1 Mark the stripes on the pot using masking tape. Cut some lengths into narrower widths to get variation in the finished design. Bear in mind that the areas covered by masking tape will remain natural terracotta.

2 Paint the body of the pot with undercoat, avoiding the fluted rim. Allow to dry completely.

3 Paint the coloured stripes with gouache paints, changing colour after each band of masking tape. Allow to dry completely.

4 Peel off the masking tape to reveal coloured stripes alternating with terracotta stripes.

5 Using the fine artist's brush and white undercoat, paint simple motifs over the stripes. When completely dry, coat with matt varnish.

Verdigris bucket

There is something irresistible about the luminous, blue-green tones of verdigris. It is a colour that always complements plants and is not difficult to reproduce on a cheap galvanized bucket. To make the rust bucket shown behind the verdigris one, follow the steps below, but substitute rust-coloured acrylic paint for the aqua paint.

MATERIALS

Galvanized bucket
Medium-grade sandpaper
Metal primer
Small decorating brush
Gold paint
Amber shellac
Artist's acrylic paint in white
  and aqua-green
Water for mixing
Natural sponge
Polyurethane matt varnish

1 Sand the bucket, then prime with metal primer. Allow to dry for 2–3 hours. Paint with gold paint and allow to dry for 2–3 hours.

2 Paint with amber shellac and allow to dry for 30 minutes. Mix white acrylic paint with aqua-green and enough water to make a liquid consistency.

3 Sponge on the verdigris paint and allow to dry for 1–2 hours. Apply a coat of varnish.

Lead chimney

The wonderful chalky tones of lead have made it a popular material for garden containers down the centuries. However, lead is incredibly heavy and very expensive, so here is a way of faking it, using a plastic, terracotta-coloured chimney and some simple paint effects.

MATERIALS

Plastic, terracotta-
  coloured chimney
Sandpaper
Acrylic primer
Large artist's brush

Emulsion (latex) paint in
  charcoal grey and white
Acrylic scumble glaze
Water
Decorating brush
Polyurethane matt varnish

1 Sand the chimney to give it a key. Paint with one coat of acrylic primer and allow to dry for 1–2 hours.

2 Apply one coat of charcoal-grey emulsion and allow to dry for 2–3 hours.

3 Tint the scumble glaze with white emulsion and thin with water. Paint over the chimney randomly. Wash over with water and allow to dry.

4 Add more of the white scumble mixture to parts of the chimney for extra colour and 'age'. Varnish with polyurethane matt varnish when dry.

White flowers and painted terracotta

There are plenty of inexpensive windowboxes available, but they do tend to look rather similar. Why not customize a bought windowbox to give it a touch of individuality? This deep blue painted windowbox creates an interesting setting for the cool white pelargonium and verbenas.

MATERIALS

45cm (18in) terracotta windowbox painted blue
Crocks (broken pots) or other suitable drainage material
Compost (soil mix)
Slow-release plant food granules

PLANTS

White pelargonium
2 variegated felicias
2 white trailing verbenas

1 Cover the base of the window box with a layer of crocks (broken pots) or similar drainage material.

2 Fill the windowbox with compost (soil mix). Add 2 teaspoons of slow-release plant food granules. Plant the pelargonium in the centre of the windowbox.

FELICIA

VERBENA

3 Plant a felicia on either side of the pelargonium at the back of the container. Plant a verbena on either side of the pelargonium at the front of the windowbox. Water well and stand in a sunny position.

PELARGONIUM

GARDENER'S TIP

White pelargoniums need regular dead-heading to look their best. Old flowerheads discolour and quickly spoil the appearance of the plant.

PLANT IN LATE SPRING OR EARLY SUMMER

Wedding fuchsias

MATERIALS

Wire basket
Sphagnum moss
Garden twine

PLANTS

3 Fuchsia *'Happy Wedding Day'*
3 *busy Lizzies (impatiens)*
(optional)
3 *white lace-cap hydrangeas*
(optional)

'Happy Wedding Day' is a modern fuchsia which produces very large, round flowers. The lax growth makes it highly suitable for use in a decorative wire basket. As its name suggests, this fuchsia is ideal for a wedding display. Other white-flowered plants can be used to make a really imposing display, and to reinforce the lively impact of the fuchsia's fresh white bells.

FUCHSIA

1 Make a hand-sized pad of sphagnum moss and start to cover the outside of the plastic pot containing the fuchsia.

2 Use a long piece of twine to start tying the moss in place. Leave the ends loose.

3 Continue working around the pot, using small pads of moss.

4 Use the long ends of the piece of twine to secure the moss as you work round the pot.

5 Completely cover the pot with moss. Repeat for the other plants. Group the pots together for a finished display.

GARDENER'S TIP

To ensure that you have a vigorous display with lots of flowers on the wedding day, you will need to stop the plants at least eight weeks before. This involves pinching out the sideshoots and growing tips with your fingers. It will encourage extra bushy growth, and the development of even more flower buds.

PLANT IN SPRING OR SUMMER

A silver and white wall basket

The helichrysum's silvery foliage and cool blue lavender flowers give a delicate colour scheme which would look good against a weathered background.

MATERIALS

30cm (12in) wall basket
Sphagnum moss
Compost (soil mix)
Slow-release plant food granules

PLANTS

2 *lavenders* (Lavandula dentata *var.* candicans)
Osteospermum *'Whirligig'*
2 Helichrysum petiolare

OSTEOSPERMUM

LAVENDER

HELICHRYSUM

GARDENER'S TIP

The lavender used in this project is fairly unusual – if you wish, you can substitute a low-growing variety such as 'Hidcote'.
Keep the helichrysum in check by pinching out its growing tips fairly regularly or it may take over the basket.

PLANT IN SPRING

1 Line the basket with moss and half-fill it with compost (soil mix).

2 Mix in a half-teaspoon of plant food granules. Plant the lavenders in each corner.

3 Plant the osteospermum in the centre of the basket then add the helichrysums on either side.

4 Angle the plants to encourage them to trail over the side of the basket. Fill with compost (soil mix). Water the basket and hang.

An informal wall basket

The strong pink of the dahlietta flower is echoed in the leaf colouring of the pink-flowered polygonums in this country-style basket. Silver thymes and white lobelias provide a gentle contrast.

MATERIALS

36cm (14in) wall basket
Sphagnum moss
Compost
Slow-release plant food granules

PLANTS

5 white lobelias
3 Polygonum 'Pink Bubbles'
2 thymes (Thymus 'Silver Queen')
1 pink dahlietta (miniature dahlia)

LOBELIA

THYME

POLYGONUM

DAHLIETTA

GARDENER'S TIP

To prevent the thyme getting leggy, trim off all the flowerheads after flowering – this will help to maintain a dense, well-shaped plant.

PLANT IN SPRING

1 Line the back and the base of the basket with moss, and position three lobelias around the side of the basket near the base.

2 Plant two of the polygonums into the side of the basket above the lobelia. Rest the root-balls on the moss, and gently feed the foliage through the basket.

3 Fill the basket with compost (soil mix). Add a half-teaspoon of slow-release plant food granules into the top of the compost. Plant the thymes into the corners of the basket, angling them so that they tumble over the sides.

4 Plant the dahlietta in the middle of the basket and the remaining polygonum in front of the dahlietta. Plant the remaining lobelias. Water well and hang in a sunny position.

A medley of pinks

DIANTHUS

PETUNIA

PELARGONIUM

In this basket-weave stone planter sugar-pink petunias are planted with ivy-leaved pelargoniums and shaggy-flowered pink dianthus with a deep-red eye. None of these plants requires much depth for its roots and, provided the plants are fed and watered regularly, they will be happy.

MATERIALS

60cm (24in) window box
Gravel
Compost (soil mix)
Slow-release plant food granules

PLANTS

2 pink-flowered ivy-leaved
  pelargoniums
3 sugar-pink petunias
6 pink dianthus

1 Fill the base of the windowbox with a layer of washed gravel or similar drainage material.

2 Fill the window box with compost (soil mix), adding in 2 teaspoons of plant food granules.

3 Plant the two pelargoniums 10cm (4in) from either end of the window box.

4 Plant the petunias, evenly spaced, along the back edge of the windowbox.

5 Plant four dianthus along the front edge, and the other two on either side of the central petunia.

6 Spread a layer of gravel around the plants; this is decorative and also helps to retain moisture. Water well and stand in a sunny position.

GARDENER'S TIP

Once the summer is over, the petunias and pelargoniums will need to be removed, but the dianthus will overwinter quite happily. Cut off any flower stems and add a fresh layer of gravel.

PLANT IN LATE SPRING OR EARLY SUMMER

In the pink

The common name for *Dianthus deltoides* is the pink. Its delightful deeply coloured flowers and silvery grey foliage work very well in a hanging basket combined with prostrate thymes, pink-flowered verbena and an osteospermum.

MATERIALS

36cm (14in) hanging basket
Sphagnum moss
Compost (soil mix)
Slow-release plant food granules

PLANTS

6 Dianthus deltoides
Osteospermum 'Pink Whirls'
Verbena 'Silver Anne'
3 thymes (Thymus 'Pink Chintz'
 or similar prostrate variety)

PINKS

THYME

VERBENA

OSTEOSPERMUM

GARDENER'S TIP

Pinch out the growing tips regularly to prevent plants such as the osteospermum growing too vigorously upwards and unbalancing the look of the basket. It will be bushier and more in scale with the other plants as a result.

PLANT IN SPRING

1 Line the bottom half of the basket with moss and fill with compost (soil mix). Plant three of the pinks into the side of the basket, resting the root-balls on the compost and feeding the leaves carefully through the wire.

2 Line the rest of the basket with moss and fill with compost (soil mix). Work a teaspoon of slow-release plant food granules into the top of the compost. Plant the osteospermum in the centre of the basket.

3 Plant the verbena to one side of the osteospermum on the edge of the basket and the thymes, evenly spaced, around the unplanted edge.

4 Plant the remaining three pinks between the thymes and the verbena. Water well and hang in a sunny position.

A sunny wall basket

MATERIALS

30cm (12in) wall basket
Sphagnum moss
Compost (soil mix)
Slow-release plant food granules

PLANTS

2 Lysimachia congestiflora
3 *Alaska nasturtiums*
3 *mixed colour African marigolds*
   (tagetes)

LYSIMACHIA

NASTURTIUM

AFRICAN
MARIGOLDS

The vibrant yellows, oranges and reds of the flowers in this basket glow richly amongst the variegated leaves of the nasturtiums. As the season progresses the underplanted lysimachia will bear deep yellow flowers and add another layer of colour.

1 Line the back of the basket and half-way up the front with moss. Plant the lysimachia by resting the root-balls on the moss and feeding the foliage between the wires.

2 Line the rest of the basket and fill with compost (soil mix), adding in a half-teaspoon of plant food granules. Plant the nasturtiums along the back.

3 Plant the African marigolds in front of the nasturtiums. Water the basket well and hang it up in a sunny spot.

GARDENER'S TIP

If you have a large area of wall to cover, group two or three wall baskets together.
This looks very effective, especially when they are planted with the same plants.

PLANT IN SPRING

Dark drama

The intense purple of the heliotrope usually dominates other plants, but here it is teamed with a selection of equally dramatic colours – *Dahlia* 'Bednall Beauty', with its purple foliage and dark red flowers, black grass and red and purple verbenas – to make a stunning display.

MATERIALS

60cm (24in) terracotta
  windowbox
Polystyrene (plastic foam) or
  other suitable drainage material
Compost (soil mix)
Slow-release plant food granules

PLANTS

Heliotrope
2 *Dahlia* 'Bednall Beauty'
Black grass (Ophiopogon
  planiscapus 'Nigrescens')
2 *purple trailing verbenas*
2 *red trailing verbenas*

BLACK GRASS

VERBENAS

DAHLIA

HELIOTROPE

1 Fill the bottom of the windowbox with broken polystyrene (plastic foam) or other suitable drainage material.

2 Fill the windowbox with compost (soil mix), adding in 3 teaspoons of slow-release plant food granules. Plant the heliotrope centrally at the back of the windowbox, gently teasing apart the roots, if necessary.

3 Plant the dahlias in the back corners of the windowbox.

4 Plant the black grass in front of the heliotrope.

5 Plant the purple verbenas at the back between the heliotrope and the dahlias.

6 Plant the red verbenas at the front in either corner. This is a large container so it is best to position it before watering. Put it where it will benefit from full sun, then water thoroughly.

GARDENER'S TIP

Dahlias can be overwintered by digging up the tubers after the first frosts, cutting the stems back to 15cm (6in) and drying them off before storing in slightly damp peat in a frost-free shed. Start into growth again in spring and plant out after all danger of frost is past.

PLANT IN LATE SPRING OR EARLY SUMMER

A cascade of lilac and silver

Petunias and violas are surrounded by a cascading curtain of variegated ground ivy and silver-leaved senecio in this softly coloured hanging basket.

MATERIALS

30cm (12in) hanging basket
Sphagnum moss
Compost (soil mix)
Slow-release plant food granules

PLANTS

3 deep blue violas
3 soft blue petunias
Variegated ground ivy (Glechoma
  hederacea *'Variegata')*
3 Senecio cineraria 'Silver Dust'

SENECIO

IVY

PETUNIA

VIOLAS

GARDENER'S TIP

If the ground ivy becomes too rampant and threatens to throttle the other plants, prune it by removing some of the stems completely and reducing the length of the others.

PLANT IN LATE SPRING OR EARLY SUMMER

1 Line the lower half of the basket with moss. Plant the violas in the side by resting the root-balls on the moss, and carefully guiding the foliage between the wires. Line the rest of the basket with moss and fill with compost (soil mix), working a teaspoon of slow-release plant food granules into the top layer.

2 Plant the three petunias, evenly spaced, in the top of the basket. Plant the ground ivy on one side to trail over the edge of the basket.

3 Plant the three senecios between the petunias. Water well and hang in a sunny position.

Scented spring planter

Lilies-of-the-valley grow very well in containers and they will thrive in the shade where their delicate scented flowers stand out amongst the greenery. Surrounding the plants with bun moss is practical as well as attractive as it will stop the soil splashing back on to the leaves and flowers during fierce spring showers.

MATERIALS

Tinware planter
Clay granules
Compost (soil mix)
Bun moss

PLANTS

6–8 pots of lily-of-the-valley

LILY OF THE VALLEY

1 Fill the bottom of the planter with 5cm (2in) of clay granules to improve drainage.

2 Cover the granules with a layer of compost (soil mix) and arrange the lily-of-the-valley plants evenly on the compost.

GARDENER'S TIP

If you want to bring your planter indoors to enjoy the scent of the flowers, use a container without drainage holes in the base, but be very careful not to overwater. Once the plants have finished flowering replant them in a pot with normal drainage holes or in the garden. They are woodland plants and will be quite happy under trees.

PLANT IN EARLY SPRING

3 Fill in around the plants with more compost (soil mix), making sure to press firmly around the plants so that they won't rock about in the wind. Now cover the compost with bun moss, fitting it snugly around the stems of the lily-of-the-valley, as this will also help keep the plants upright.

Woodland garden

You do not need your own woodland area for this garden, just a shady corner and an attractive container to hold a selection of plants that thrive in damp shade. The plants are buried in bark chippings in their pots and will relish these conditions as they closely imitate their natural habitat.

BLUEBELL

ANEMONE
BLANDA

FERNS

PLANTS

Pot of bluebells
3 hardy ferns
Pot of Anemone blanda

1 Fill the container three-quarters full with bark chippings. Plant your largest pot (in this case the bluebells) first. Scoop a hollow in the bark and position the pot so that the base of the leaves is approximately 5cm (2in) below the rim of the container.

2 Cover the pot with bark so that the plastic is no longer visible and the plant is surrounded by chippings.

3 Arrange the ferns so that they relate attractively to one another. Fill the spaces between the ferns with bark.

4 Add the *Anemone blanda* at the front of the container where its flowers will be seen to best advantage, and then top up the whole arrangement with bark. Stand the container in light shade and water.

GARDENER'S TIP

After the bluebells and anemones have finished flowering, lift them out of the container in their pots and set them aside in a shady corner to rest. They can be replaced by other woodland plants such as wild strawberries or periwinkle.

PLANT IN EARLY SPRING

A garland of spring flowers

Miniature daffodils, deep blue pansies, yellow polyanthus and variegated ivy are planted together to make a hanging basket that will flower for many weeks in early spring, lifting the spirits with its fresh colours and delicate woodland charm.

MATERIALS

30cm (12in) hanging basket
Sphagnum moss
Compost (soil mix)
Slow-release plant food granules

PLANTS

3 variegated ivies
5 miniature daffodil bulbs 'Tête-à-Tête' or similar, or a pot of daffodils in bud
3 blue pansies
2 yellow polyanthus

POLYANTHUS

IVY

PANSY

MINIATURE DAFFODIL

1 Line the lower half of the basket with moss.

3 Line the rest of the basket with moss and add a layer of compost (soil mix) to the bottom of the basket. Push the daffodil bulbs into the compost.

5 Plant the polyanthus between the pansies. Water the basket and hang in sun or shade. If planting daffodils in bud, remove them from the pot and place in the centre of the basket before arranging the ivies and filling with compost (soil mix).

2 Plant the ivies into the side of the basket by resting the root-balls on the moss, and guiding the foliage through the basket so that it will trail down.

4 Fill the remainder of the basket with compost (soil mix), working a teaspoon of slow-release plant food granules into the top layer. Plant the pansies, evenly spaced, in the top of the basket.

GARDENER'S TIP

When dismantling the arrangement, plant the variegated ivies in the garden. They look particularly good tumbling over walls, or threading their way through and linking established shrubs. Prune hard if they get out of hand and become too invasive.

PLANT IN AUTUMN IF GROWING DAFFODILS FROM BULBS; IN LATE WINTER OR EARLY SPRING FOR READY-GROWN DAFFODILS

Foliage basket

An old basket makes an ideal container for this interesting group of foliage plants. The different leaf shapes and colours are emphasized when they are grouped together. Including flowers would detract from the architectural quality of the plants.

MATERIALS

30cm (12in) basket
Sphagnum moss
Loam-based compost (soil mix)
Slow-release plant food granules
Bark chippings

PLANTS

Phormium tenax
Mexican orange blossom
(Choisya ternata)
Carex brunnea 'Variegata'

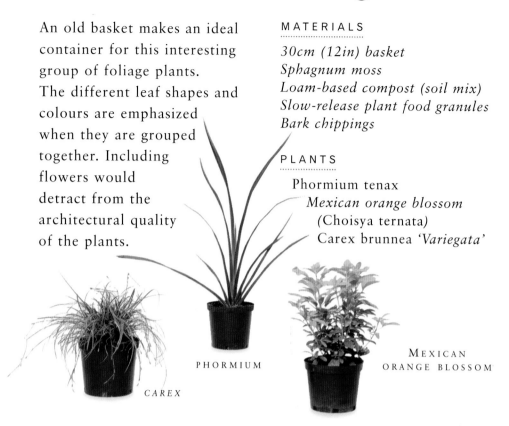

PHORMIUM

MEXICAN
ORANGE BLOSSOM

CAREX

GARDENER'S TIP

A planted basket makes an ideal gift for a friend, especially when you have chosen the plants yourself. Include a label, giving the names of the plants and how to care for them.

PLANT AT ANY TIME OF THE YEAR

1 Line the basket with moss. Place the phormium at the back and position the orange blossom next to it.

2 Add the carex and fill between the plants with compost (soil mix) enriched with a tablespoon of slow-release plant food granules.

3 Mulch around the plants with bark chippings. Water well and place in partial shade.

Layers of flowers

MATERIALS

36 cm (14 in) fibre windowbox
Drainage material
Compost (soil mix)
Slow-release plant food granules

PLANTS

2 white tobacco plants
Variegated Pelargonium
  'l'Elégante'
2 pink busy Lizzies (impatiens)
3 white lobelias

This windowbox is unusual as the colours are in distinct layers, with upright white flowering tobacco above pink busy Lizzies, and tumbling white variegated pelargonium and lobelias. The fibre windowbox is concealed by a decorative twig container.

LOBELIAS

TOBACCO

PELARGONIUM

BUSY LIZZIE

1 Put some drainage material in the base of the windowbox; fill with compost (soil mix), mixing in 2 teaspoons of plant food granules. Plant the flowering tobacco near the back edge.

2 Plant the pelargonium at the front of the windowbox, in the centre.

3 Plant the busy Lizzies at each end of the windowbox.

4 Plant one of the lobelias between the flowering tobacco, and the other two on either side of the pelargonium.

GARDENER'S TIP

Somehow, rogue blue lobelias have appeared among the white plants. This sort of thing often happens in gardening and, as in this case, the accidental addition can turn out well.

PLANT IN SPRING

Full of cheer

Vivid red pelargoniums and verbenas are combined with cheerful yellow bidens and soft green helichrysums in this planter, which brightens the exterior of an old barn.

MATERIALS

76cm (30in) plastic windowbox
Compost (soil mix)
Slow-release plant food granules

PLANTS

3 scarlet pelargoniums
2 Bidens ferulifolia
2 red trailing verbenas
2 Helichrysum petiolare 'Aureum'

HELICHRYSUM

BIDENS

PELARGONIUM

VERBENA

GARDENER'S TIP

Regular dead-heading and an occasional foliar feed will keep the pelargoniums flowering prolifically all summer.

PLANT IN SPRING

1 The easiest way to make drainage holes in a plastic planter is with an electric drill.

2 Fill the windowbox with compost (soil mix), working in 2 teaspoons of slow-release plant food granules.

3 Plant the pelargoniums, evenly spaced, in the windowbox.

4 Plant the two bidens on either side of the central pelargonium to spill over the front of the planter.

5 Plant the two verbenas on either side of the central pelargonium towards the back of the planter.

6 Plant the helichrysums in the front corners. Water thoroughly and stand the box in a sunny position.

A wild one

Native plants are those that have grown naturally in the countryside for thousands of years. Some of the most colourful ones are cornfield flowers, but many are quite rare now. To enjoy them this summer, sow a pot full of wild flowers to stand on your doorstep.

MATERIALS

Pebbles
Very large flower pot
Garden soil

PLANTS

Packet of wild flower seeds

FLOWER POT

WILD FLOWER SEEDS

PEBBLES

GARDEN SOIL

1 Put a few pebbles in the base of the pot for drainage.

2 Fill the pot with garden soil, taking out any bits of roots or large stones.

3 Make sure the surface is level, then sprinkle a large pinch of flower seeds evenly on top.

4 Cover the seeds lightly with soil, just so you can't see them any more, and water them in with a gentle sprinkle.

GARDENER'S TIP

Remember to keep watering as the flowers grow!
Pots need much more watering than beds because the water drains away.

PLANT IN EARLY SPRING

A pastel composition

Pure white pelargonium blooms emerge from a sea of blue felicias, pinky-blue brachycome daisies and verbenas in this romantic basket.

VERBENA

BRACHYCOME

FELICIA

PELARGONIUM

MATERIALS

36cm (14in) hanging basket
Sphagnum moss
Compost (soil mix)
Slow-release plant food granules

PLANTS

2 pink verbenas
2 Brachycome 'Pink Mist'
Blue felicia
White pelargonium

1 Line the basket with moss and fill with compost (soil mix). Work a teaspoon of plant food granules into the top layer.

2 Plant the verbenas opposite each other at the edge of the basket, so that the foliage will tumble over the sides.

3 Plant the brachycome daisies around the edge of the basket. Plant the felicia off-centre in the middle of the basket.

4 Plant the pelargonium off-centre in the remaining space in the middle of the basket. Water thoroughly and hang in a sunny position.

GARDENER'S TIP

White pelargonium flowers discolour as they age; be sure to pick them off to keep the basket looking at its best.

PLANT IN LATE SPRING OR EARLY SUMMER

Daisy chains

The soft yellow of the marguerites' flowers is emphasized by combining them with yellow-leaved helichrysum and bright blue felicia in this summery basket.

MARGUERITE

HELICHRYSUM

FELICIA

MATERIALS

40cm (16in) hanging basket
Sphagnum moss
Compost (soil mix)
Slow-release plant food granules

PLANTS

3 variegated felicias
3 yellow marguerites
  (argyranthemums)
3 Helichrysum petiolare 'Aureum'

GARDENER'S TIP

Pinch out the growing tips of the marguerites regularly to encourage bushy plants.

PLANT IN LATE SPRING OR EARLY SUMMER

1 Line the lower half of the basket with moss. Plant the felicias into the sides of the basket by resting the root-balls on the moss, and carefully guiding the foliage through the wires.

2 Line the rest of the basket with moss. Fill with compost (soil mix), working a teaspoon of plant food granules into the top layer. Plant the marguerites in the top of the basket.

3 Plant the helichrysums between the marguerites, angling the plants to encourage them to grow over the edge of the basket. Water well and hang in full or partial sun.

Scented pelargoniums

There is a wonderful variation in leaf size, shape and colouring, as well as an incredible diversity of scents, amongst the *Pelargonium* family. Choose the fragrances you like best and put the plants where you will brush against them to release their fragrance.

MATERIALS

40cm (16in) terracotta windowbox
Crocks (china) or other suitable drainage material
Compost (soil mix)
Slow-release plant food granules

PLANTS

4 scented-leaf pelargoniums

PELARGONIUMS

GARDENER'S TIP

During the summer, pick and dry the leaves of these pelargoniums for use in pot-pourri or in muslin bags to scent linen. If you have a greenhouse or conservatory, move the windowbox inside for the winter and water sparingly until spring.

PLANT IN SPRING

1 Cover the base of the window-box with crocks (broken pots) or other suitable drainage material. Fill with compost (soil mix), working in 2 teaspoons of slow-release plant food granules. Plant the first pelargonium at the right-hand end of the container.

2 Choose a plant with contrasting leaf colour and shape, and place this next to the first pelargonium towards the front edge of the windowbox.

3 Plant the third pelargonium behind the second.

4 Finally, plant the fourth pelargonium at the left-hand end of the container. Water well and position in full or partial sun.

A butterfly garden

We should all do our bit to encourage butterflies into our gardens and this windowbox filled with sedum, marjoram, thyme and origanum should prove irresistible. All these plants are perennials and can be over-wintered in the windowbox.

MATERIALS

60cm (24in) stone windowbox
Crocks (broken pots) or other
* suitable drainage material*
Compost (soil mix)
Slow-release plant food granules

PLANTS

Sedum 'Ruby Glow'
Marjoram
Lemon thyme (Thymus
  citriodorus)
Common thyme (Thymus
  vulgaris)
Origanum

LEMON
THYME

ORIGANUM

MARJORAM

COMMON
THYME

SEDUM

GARDENER'S TIP

You can imitate the look of an old stone windowbox by painting a new one with a dilute mixture of liquid seaweed plant food and water. This encourages moss to grow and ages the stone.

PLANT IN SPRING

1 Cover the base of the window box with a layer of crocks (broken pots). Fill with compost (soil mix), mixing in 3 teaspoons of slow-release plant food granules.

2 Plant the sedum off-centre to the left of the windowbox and the marjoram to the left of the sedum.

3 Plant the lemon thyme in the centre front and the common thyme in the back right-hand corner of the container.

4 Plant the origanum in the front right-hand corner of the windowbox. Water well and place in a sunny position.

Star-jasmine in a villandry planter

The soft, seductive scent of the star-jasmine makes this a perfect container to place by the side of a door where the scent will be appreciated by all who pass through.

STAR-
JASMINE

MATERIALS

50cm (20in) villandry planter or similar, preferably self-watering
Equal mix loam-based compost (soil mix) and standard compost
Slow-release plant food granules
Bark chippings

PLANTS

Star-jasmine (Trachelospermum jasminoides)

GARDENER'S TIP

Use a plastic liner inside all large planters. It is easier to remove the liner when replanting rather than dismantle the entire container.

PLANT IN LATE SPRING OR EARLY SUMMER

1 Feed the wicks through the holes in the base of the liner.

2 Fill the water reservoir in the base of the planter to the top of the overflow pipe, and place the liner inside the planter.

3 Fill the bottom of the liner with compost (soil mix) while pulling through the wicks so that they reach the level of the roots.

4 Remove the jasmine from its pot, gently tease the roots loose and stand it in the planter.

NOTE *Steps 1–3 are for self-watering planters only.*

5 Add compost (soil mix) and firm it around the root-ball of the jasmine. Scatter 2 tablespoons of plant food granules on the surface, and gently work them into the top layer of compost with the trowel.

6 Mulch around the plant with a layer of bark chippings, then water. Check the reservoir of the self-watering container once a week and top up if necessary. Conventional pots should be watered daily in the early morning or evening during hot weather.

Shady corner

Shady corners are often thought of as problematical, when in fact there is a wealth of wonderful plants that thrive in these situations, such as the hosta, hydrangea and fern used in this arrangement.

MATERIALS

3 terracotta pots of various sizes
Crocks (broken pots) or other suitable drainage material
Composted manure
Equal mix standard compost (soil mix) and loam-based compost

PLANTS

Hosta sieboldiana elegans
Variegated hydrangea
Polystichum fern

HYDRANGEA

POLYSTICHUM

HOSTA

GARDENER'S TIP

The hosta is a beautiful foliage plant much loved by slugs and snails which chew unsightly holes in the leaves. To prevent this, smear a broad band of petroleum jelly below the rim of the container and the leaves will remain untouched.

PLANT AT ANY TIME OF THE YEAR

2 Plant the fern in a terracotta pot slightly larger than its existing pot. It should not need transplanting for 2–3 years.

1 Plant the hosta in a pot large enough for its bulky root system, and with space for further growth. Place crocks (broken pots) at the bottom of the pot and then put in a layer of manure before adding the potting compost (soil mix). Follow this procedure with the hydrangea as well.

3 The hydrangea makes a great deal of growth during the summer and could get very top-heavy. Plant in a sturdy pot with plenty of space for root growth.

A trough of alpines

A selection of easy-to-grow alpine plants is grouped in a basket-weave stone planter to create a miniature garden. The mulch of gravel is both attractive and practical as it prevents soil splashing on to the leaves of the plants.

MATERIALS

40cm (16in) stone trough
Crocks (broken pots)
Compost (soil mix)
Slow-release plant food granules
Gravel

PLANTS

Sempervivum
Alpine aquilegia
White rock rose (helianthemum)
Papaver alpinum
Alpine phlox
Pink saxifrage
White saxifrage

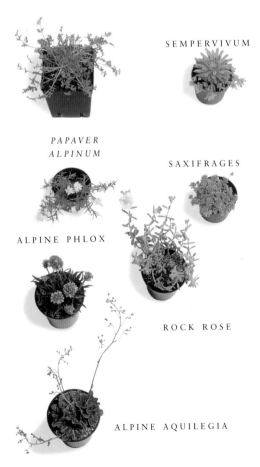

SEMPERVIVUM

PAPAVER ALPINUM

SAXIFRAGES

ALPINE PHLOX

ROCK ROSE

ALPINE AQUILEGIA

1 Cover the base of the trough with crocks (broken pots). Fill the container with compost (soil mix), working in a teaspoon of plant food granules and extra gravel for improved drainage.

2 Arrange the plants, still in their pots, in the trough to decide on the most attractive arrangement. Complete the planting, working across the trough.

3 Scatter a good layer of gravel around the plants. Water thoroughly and stand in a sunny position.

GARDENER'S TIP

Tidy the trough once a month, removing dead flowerheads and leaves, adding more gravel if necessary. A trough like this will last a number of years before it needs replanting.

PLANT IN SPRING

The apothecary's box

Many plants have healing qualities and, while they should always be used with caution, some of the more commonly used herbs have been successful country remedies for centuries.

MATERIALS

Wooden trug
Crocks (broken pots) or other
  suitable drainage material
Compost (soil mix)
Pelleted chicken manure

FENNEL

CHAMOMILE

LAVENDER

MARIGOLD

ROSEMARY

FEVERFEW

PLANTS

Lavender – for relaxation
Rosemary – for healthy hair
  and scalp
Chamomile – for restful sleep
Fennel – for digestion
Feverfew – for migraine
3 pot marigolds (calendula) –
  for healing

1 Place drainage material in the trug and fill with compost (soil mix), working in 2 teaspoons of fertilizer. Plant a central lavender.

2 Plant the rosemary in the front right-hand corner of the trug.

3 Plant the chamomile in the back left-hand corner.

4 Plant the fennel in the back right-hand corner.

5 Plant the feverfew in the front left-hand corner.

6 Plant the marigolds in the remaining spaces. Water well and stand in full or partial sun.

GARDENER'S TIP

Herbs should not be used to treat any medical condition without first checking with your medical practitioner.

PLANT IN THE SPRING

Foliage wall pot

The bushy growth of *Fuchsia magellanica* 'Alba Variegata' is ideal for displaying as a crown of leafy hair in a head-shaped wall pot. This copy of an ancient Grecian head will add a classical touch to a modern garden.

FUCHSIA

MATERIALS

Grecian head wall pot
Expanded clay granules

PLANTS

Fuchsia magellanica *'Alba Variegata'*

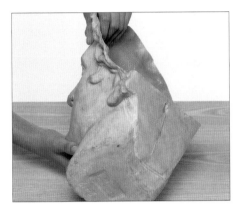

1 Check that the wall pot has a hook or can be hung up. The hanging point will need to be sufficiently strong to carry the weight of a moist pot.

2 Add expanded clay granules to the base of the wall pot to lift the top of the plant to the right level.

3 Place the plant in its pot inside the wall pot.

4 Arrange the foliage to make a convincing leafy crown of hair for the head.

GARDENER'S TIP

Check the base of the pot for drainage holes. If there are no holes, you will need to remove the pot each time you water it, allowing the compost to drain before replacing it.

PLANT AT ANY TIME OF YEAR

Filigree foliage

The purply-black leaves of this heuchera are all the more stunning when surrounded by the delicate silver-and-green filigree foliage of senecio, the tender *Lavandula pinnata* and the soft lilac-coloured flowers of the bacopa and the brachycome daisies. The plants are grown in a white plastic planter which is concealed inside an elegant wooden windowbox.

MATERIALS

76cm (30in) plastic windowbox
Compost (soil mix)
Slow-release plant food granules
90cm (3ft) wooden windowbox
  (optional)

PLANTS

Heuchera 'Palace Purple'
2 lavenders
2 blue brachycome daisies
3 Senecio cineraria 'Silver Dust'
2 blue bacopa

SENECIO

LAVENDER

BRACHYCOME

BACOPA

HEUCHERA

1 Check drainage holes are open in the base of the planter and, if not, drill or punch them out. Fill the windowbox with compost (soil mix), mixing in 2 teaspoons of plant food granules. Plant the heuchera in the centre.

2 Plant the two lavenders on either side of the heuchera.

3 Plant the two brachycome daisies at each end of the windowbox.

4 Place the three senecios at the front of the box between the brachycomes.

5 Plant the two bacopa between the senecio and the heuchera.

6 Water thoroughly and lift into place in the wooden window-box, if using. Place in full or partial sun.

GARDENER'S TIP

Wooden windowboxes can be assembled so they are self-watering where access is difficult for daily watering. A variety of self-watering containers are available and come with full instructions for their use.

PLANT IN SPRING

Indoor table-top garden

Many indoor plants have dramatically coloured flowers and foliage. In this arrangement the purple flowers of the African violet are echoed by the velvety leaves of the gynura. The delicate fronds of the maidenhair fern and the dark green foliage of the button fern add interest with their contrasting shape and colour.

MATERIALS

30cm (12in) terracotta seed tray
Crocks (broken pots)
Houseplant compost (soil mix)
Slow-release plant food granules
Clay granules

PLANTS

Maidenhair fern (adiantum)
African violet (saintpaulia)
Gynura
Button fern (Pellaea rotundifolia)

AFRICAN VIOLET

MAIDENHAIR FERN

GARDENER'S TIP

Terracotta transmits moisture and will mark a table-top if it is in direct contact with it. Cut 2.5 cm (1in) sections from a cork and glue them to the four corners of the seed tray. A plastic tray smaller than the seed tray can then be slipped underneath it to catch any drips.

PLANT AT ANY TIME
OF THE YEAR

1 Cover the drainage holes in the bottom of the seed tray with crocks (broken pots).

2 Arrange the plants before removing them from their pots. Plant the tallest plant first, then add the others around it.

3 Fill any gaps with compost (soil mix) and scatter a table-spoon of plant food granules on the surface. Mulch between the plants with clay granules to help retain moisture. Water and place in a light position, but out of direct sunlight. Spray regularly with water.

Bottle it up

Bottle gardens are great fun to make, and if you choose a stoppered bottle you will probably be able to grow some of those tricky plants that demand very high humidity. Don't worry too much about choosing the right plants, however. If you are prepared to replace plants when they outgrow their space, just concentrate on the plants that please you. You will have to improvise tools for your bottle garden by lashing old pieces of cutlery to garden canes.

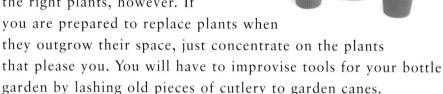

SMALL FOLIAGE PLANTS

MATERIALS

Large glass bottle with cork
Fine gravel
Paper or thin cardboard
Charcoal
Compost (soil mix)
Knife, fork, spoon and cotton reel attached to canes

PLANTS

Small foliage plants

1 Place some fine gravel in the bottom of the bottle. If the neck is narrow you can make yourself a funnel from paper or thin cardboard to scatter it evenly over the base.

2 Add a thin layer of charcoal. This will help to absorb impurities and reduce the risk of the bottle smelling if there is too much moisture.

3 Spread a layer of compost (soil mix) over the base, and level it. Using your improvised trowel, make a hole for the plant.

4 Firm each plant in well. If you can't reach with your hand, use a cotton reel pushed on to the end of a cane to tamp down the compost (soil mix).

5 Work around the whole bottle until it is fully planted. Then mist the plants. Aim the spray at the sides of the bottle if compost (soil mix) is clinging to the glass and spoiling the effect. Leave the plants and compost moist but not soaking wet.

6 If using a stoppered bottle you will have to balance the atmosphere over a week or two. You may need to keep inserting or removing the cork for periods (see opposite).

GARDENER'S TIP

Place the cork firmly in position and leave it for a day or two. Some misting of the glass, especially in the morning, is quite normal – but if it never clears there is too much moisture, so leave the cork off for a day and try again. If no condensation appears at all, it is probably too dry – mist again, then return the cork. It will take trial and error at first, but once the atmosphere is balanced you can leave the bottle for months without attention, although you will have to prune or remove plants that become too large.

PLANT IN SPRING

Palm court

1 Unless your palm is small, choose a large pot. As it will be conspicuous, choose an attractive, decorative one that does the plant justice. Start by placing a layer of polystyrene (plastic foam) or other drainage material in the bottom.

Palms look graceful and elegant. They usually look best in isolation or among other palms, rather than in a group of mixed plants. Display them so that their classic shape can be appreciated. Allow these aristocrats space to make a statement.

MATERIALS

Decorative pot with drainage hole
Polystyrene (plastic foam) or other suitable
  drainage material
Compost (soil mix), loam-based if plant is large
Bark chippings

PLANT

Palm, appropriate for size of pot

PALM

2 Stand the palm in the pot and surround the root-ball with container compost (soil mix), pressing it firmly around the plant. Scatter a tablespoon of plant food granules on the surface.

3 Cover the compost (soil mix) with a layer of bark and water. Place in a position that receives good light, but no more than a couple of hours of direct sunlight each day. Water regularly during growing season, but allow the compost to dry out between waterings during the winter.

GARDENER'S TIP

Palms can look splendid in isolation, but they usually look more impressive in a collection. Display plants of different sizes to add interest, and place small ones on pedestals in front of taller ones in large pots. Like most houseplants, the palm will benefit from being stood outside during warm summer rain. A good soaking shower removes dust from the leaves and gives the plant the benefit of a drink of untreated water.

PLANT IN SPRING

Mixed blessings

A bowl of mixed plants almost always looks better than the same number dotted around in individual pots. Garden centres and florists often sell mixed bowls, but you can probably make one more cheaply using a container that you already have – and you can ring the changes with different plants.

FOLIAGE AND
FLOWERING PLANTS

MATERIALS

Bowl with drainage hole
Crocks (broken pots)
Compost (soil mix)
Spare pot the same size as centrepiece plant pot

PLANTS

Collection of mixed foliage and flowering plants

1 Cover the drainage hole with crocks (broken pots). Part-fill the container with compost (soil mix).

2 It is a good idea to have a showy centrepiece plant – insert an empty pot temporarily so that you are sure to leave enough space.

3 Place the other plants around the centrepiece, rearranging them as necessary while still in their pots. Do not start planting until you are happy with the results.

GARDENER'S TIP

For a lively, varied mix use a combination of small bushy, vertical, and trailing plants. Tradescantias are a good choice for the last category, particularly since they come in a wide range of bright colours, including greens, creams and bronze.

PLANT AT ANY TIME OF YEAR

4 Remove the plants from their pots and plant. Finally, insert the centrepiece. If it is likely to be a long-term occupant, remove it from its pot. If you are likely to have to replace it after a few weeks – as is common with flowering plants once they finish blooming – keep it in its container.

Start a collection

Once houseplants become more of a consuming hobby than a passing pleasure, you will begin to look for more ways to feed your passion. One option is to start a collection of a particular type of plants, whether a large and diverse group such as cacti, or a smaller, interesting group like saintpaulias (African violets).

SAINTPAULIAS

MATERIALS

Baskets or containers of various sizes
Florist's foam
Moss

PLANTS

Collection of plants, such as saintpaulias (African violets)

1 Start by grouping your plants to find an arrangement that pleases you.

2 The design will look more interesting if you can create a cascade effect using florist's foam to build up different levels.

3 Build up the back of the display on florist's foam first.

4 Fill in the space in front in steps. Try the plants for size so that you can use more foam beneath the pots if needed.

PLANT IN EARLY SPRING

5 Arrange the plants to look as though they could be growing as a natural group and not in straight rows. Fill the spaces between the pots with moss.

Orchid basket

MILTONIA

PLANTS

Miltonia or phalaenopsis orchid

Orchids are no longer the rare exotic plants that they used to be and most garden centres now stock some. A few inexpensive materials and a little time will create a stylish container to show these lovely flowers at their very best.

MATERIALS

Plastic-lined twig basket, 15cm (6in) diameter
Gravel
Sphagnum moss
3 x 40cm (16in) canes
Raffia

1 Pour a 2.5cm (1in) layer of gravel into the base of the basket and line with moss.

2 Slip the orchid (still in its pot) into the basket.

3 Push the canes into the moss at the edge of the basket so that they are held firmly in place.

4 Tie a length of raffia between each cane, finishing off with a neat knot.

GARDENER'S TIP

Orchids do not like to stand in water, but they do like a humid atmosphere. A layer of gravel underneath the pot acts as a reservoir for excess water which creates humidity. The orchid will also benefit from being sprayed with water.

PLANT AT ANY TIME OF THE YEAR

Dramatic datura

The angel's trumpet or *Datura* (strictly speaking, it should now be known as *Brugmansia*), a popular conservatory plant, will grow enormous in time, provided it is planted in a large container and given regular food and water. The plant will benefit from a period outdoors during the summer, but will grow indoors for the rest of the year.

MATERIALS

Deep planter, at least 40cm (16in) diameter
Polystyrene (plastic foam) or similar drainage material
Gloves
Equal mix loam-based compost (soil mix) and container compost
Slow-release plant food granules

PLANTS

Angel's trumpet (Brugmansia suaveolens)
4 white busy lizzies (impatiens)

ANGEL'S TRUMPET

BUSY LIZZIE

1 Fill the base of the container with lightweight polystyrene (plastic foam) or similar drainage material. Wear gloves to lift the angel's trumpet into the container.

2 Pour compost (soil mix) round the edges of the plant, pressing down firmly around the root-ball. Scatter 2 tablespoons of plant food granules on the surface.

3 Plant the busy Lizzies around the base of the angel's trumpet, and remember to water frequently.

GARDENER'S TIP

All parts of the angel's trumpet are poisonous, and it should be handled with care. Standing it outside in summer is recommended as the scent of the flowers can have a narcotic effect in confined spaces. It is not recommended in households with small children. While it is sensible to be cautious, it is also a fact that many commonly cultivated plants are poisonous. For example, with the exception of its tubers, the potato plant is poisonous, as are dieffenbachia and oleander.

PLANT IN SPRING

Plant guide

TREES AND SHRUBS FOR CONTAINERS

Acer palmatum
Apple (dwarf)
Bay
Berberis thunbergii 'Atropurpurea Nana',
    B. darwinii
Box
Camellia
Ceratostigma plumbaginoides
Chamaecyparis pisifera
Choisya ternata
x *Citrofortunella microcarpa**
Convolvulus cneorum
Cordyline*
Cotoneaster conspicuus
Datura*
Euonymus fortunei
Fuchsia
Hebe
Holly
Hydrangea
Lantana*
Lavender
Potentilla
Rhododendron
Rosemary
Rose
Skimmia

CLIMBERS FOR CONTAINERS

Bougainvillea*
Clematis alpina, C. macropetala
*Cobaea scandens**
Gynura*
Ivy
Jasmine
Stephanotis*
Thunbergia alata
Trachelospermum jasminoides

HARDY PLANTS FOR PERMANENT PLANTING IN CONTAINERS

Anemone blanda
Aquilegia alpina
Arabis ferdinandi-coburgi 'Variegata'
Asplenium crispum
Athyrium niponicum
Berberis thunbergii 'Atropurpurea Nana',
    B. darwinii
Bergenia
Box
Ceratostigma plumbaginoides
Chamaecyparis pisifera 'Filifera Aurea', 'Sungold'
Choisya ternata
Convolvulus cneorum
Cotoneaster conspicuus
Crocus
Day lily
Dianthus
Dryopteris filix-mas
Euonymus fortunei 'Emerald and Gold'
Euphorbia
Foxglove
Hebe
Helianthemum
Heuchera 'Palace Purple', 'Bressingham Bronze'
Holly
Hosta
Hydrangea
Inula
Iris reticulata
Ivy
Lamium
Lavender
Lily-of-the-valley
Narcissus
Nepeta mussinii
Ophiopogon planiscapus 'Nigrescens'
Pachysandra terminalis
Polygonum affine

Polystichum acrostichoides
Potentilla
Primula auricula
Rosemary
Salix alpina
Sedum ewersii
Sedum 'Ruby Glow'
Sempervivum
Skimmia japonica 'Rubella'
Thyme
Trachelospermum jasminoides
Veronica peduncularis
Vinca minor

TRAILING PLANTS FOR HANGING BASKETS

Ageratum*
*Begonia semperflorens**
*Bidens ferulifolia**
Brachyscome iberidifolia
*Campanula isophylla**
*Chaenorhinum glareosum**
*Convolvulus sabatius**
Erigeron mucronatus
Felicia*
Fuchsia (lax varieties)*
Gazania*
Glechoma hederacea
*Helichrysum petiolare**
Lampranthus*
Lantana*
Lobelia*
*Lotus berthelotii**
Lysimachia nummularia
Nasturtium
Osteospermum*
Pelargonium*
Petunia*
Sedum ewersii
*Senecio maritima**
Sweet peas
Verbena*
Vinca minor

SPRING-FLOWERING PLANTS FOR CONTAINERS

Anagallis
Anemone blanda
Aquilegia
Arabis ferdinandi-coburgi 'Variegata'
Bluebells
Crocus
Day lily
Euphorbia
Forget-me-not
Iris reticulata
Lily-of-the-valley
Narcissus
Polyanthus
Primroses
Primula auricula
Snowdrops
Tulips
Vinca minor
Viola
Wallflower

AUTUMN AND WINTER COLOUR

Arabis ferdinandi-coburgi 'Variegata'
Berberis thunbergii 'Atropurpurea Nana', *B. darwinii*
Bergenia
Ceratostigma plumbaginoides
Chamaecyparis pisifera 'Sungold'
Convolvulus cneorum
Euonymus fortunei
Euphorbia
Ferns
Heuchera 'Palace Purple', 'Bressingham Bronze'
Hakonechloa macra 'Alboaurea'
Hebe
Holly
Iris unguicularis
Ivy
Pachysandra terminalis
Polygonum affine
Salvia greggii
Sedum 'Ruby Glow'
Vinca minor

PLANTS FOR SHADE

Anemone blanda
Begonia semperflorens
Bergenia
Box
Campanula isophylla
Chamaecyparis pisifera
Digitalis
Euonymous
Euphorbia
Ferns
Glechoma hederacea
Heuchera
Holly
Hosta
Hydrangea
Impatiens*
Ivy
Lily-of-the-valley
Narcissus
Ophiopogon planiscapus
Pachysandra terminalis
Primrose
Primula auricula
Skimmia
Sorrel
Thunbergia alata
Trachelospermum jasminoides
Vinca minor
Viola

PLANTS FOR HOT CONDITIONS

Aloe*
Alyssum
Argyranthemum*
Arundinaria pygmaea
*Crassula ovata**
Diascia*
*Erigeron mucronatus**
Gazania*
Hakonechloa macra 'Aureola'
Helianthemum
Inula
Lavender
*Lotus berthelotii**
Mesembryanthemum
Osteospermum*

PLANTS WITH DECORATIVE FOLIAGE

Berberis thunbergii
Bergenia
Chamaecyparis pisifera
Choisya ternata

Convolvulus cneorum
Euonymus fortunei
Euphorbia
Fuchsia magellanica
Glechoma hederacea
Hebe
Hedera helix 'Hibernica'
*Helichrysum petiolare**
Heuchera
Holly
Hosta 'Blue Moon'
*Lotus berthelotii**
Lysimachia nummularia
Nasturtium 'Alaska'
Pachysandra terminalis
Pelargonium, ivy-leaved
Salvia officinalis
Senecio maritima
Thymus 'Silver Queen', 'Archer's Gold'
Vinca minor

FRAGRANT PLANTS

Alyssum
*Bidens atrosanguinea**
Cheiranthus
Choisya ternata
x *Citrofortunella microcarpa**
Dianthus
Heliotrope
Jasmine
Lavender
Lilies
Lily-of-the-valley
Nicotiana
Pelargonium, scented-leaved varieties*
Rosemary
Sweet pea
Thyme
Trachelospermum jasminoides
Viola odorata

Annuals and bedding plants

Annuals and bedding plants provide instant colour in the garden. They brighten the summer in towns and cities all over the world, enlivening planters and windowboxes, and if you have room they are well worth planting in a bed on their own or among the permanent plants in the herbaceous or mixed border.

RIGHT: *Here a windowbox is used to stunning effect with a colour-coordinated display of bedding plants.*

ABOVE: *Annuals and bedding plants are often used to fill in the gaps in a border of more established plants.*

Species _____
Sown _____ Planted out _____

Species _____
Sown _____ Planted out _____

Species _____
Sown _____ Planted out _____

Species _____
Sown _____ Planted out _____

Species _____
Sown _____ Planted out _____

Species _____
Sown _____ Planted out _____

Species _____
Sown _____ Planted out _____

Species _____
Sown _____ Planted out _____

Species _____
Sown _____ Planted out _____

Species _____
Sown _____ Planted out _____

Species _____
Sown _____ Planted out _____

Species _____
Sown _____ Planted out _____

Bulbs and tubers

The bulbs of spring are one of the first signs that the wheel of the seasons has turned and that warmer summer days are on their way. There is something charming about these early flowers, the yellow of the winter aconites, the nodding heads of the snowdrops and the teasing upright crocuses opening their heads to receive the sun's rays then closing up when it goes behind the clouds. Daffodils and narcissus are the most spectacular bulbs, covering gardens with yellow fields of colour. But there are also summer bulbs such as lilies, galtonias, scillas and chionodoxas. Then there are also the tubers, gladioli, begonias and, most important of all, the dahlias.

RIGHT: *Hyacinths, one of the best loved and popular bulbs, often grown as gifts at Christmas time as a foretaste of the coming spring.*

Species .... Year .... Year .... Year ....

Source .... Fed ....

Planted .... Divided ....

Species ....

Source .... Fed ....

Planted .... Divided ....

Species ....

Source .... Fed ....

Planted .... Divided ....

Species ....

Source .... Fed ....

Planted .... Divided ....

Species .... Year .... Year .... Year ....

Source .... Fed ....

Planted .... Divided ....

Species ....

Source .... Fed ....

Planted .... Divided ....

Species ....

Source .... Fed ....

Planted .... Divided ....

Species ....

Source .... Fed ....

Planted .... Divided ....

ABOVE: *What you should look for when buying tubers: a healthy pot tuber (left) and a healthy tuber (right).*

Species ....   Year .... Year .... Year ....

....

Source ....   Fed ....

Planted ....   Divided ....

Species ....

....

Source ....   Fed ....

Planted ....   Divided ....

Species ....

....

Source ....   Fed ....

Planted ....   Divided ....

Species ....

....

Source ....   Fed ....

Planted ....   Divided ....

ABOVE: *Plastic pots are surprisingly acceptable if the flowers are stunning, such as these vibrant spring bulbs.*

OPPOSITE: *Place pots of L. regale lilies near seats to enjoy the fragrance to the full.*

Seeds

If you have the patience, raising plants from seeds will not only save you money, but can be an immensely satisfying process. If you are lucky enough to have a greenhouse, you will be able to grow almost all the plants you need, but even without one, many will grow quite happily, either outside, in the case of hardy varieties, or on a window-sill indoors.

RIGHT: *If your seeds fail, you can usually buy replacement seedlings from a commercial greenhouse or garden centre.*

	Year	Year	Year
Type	Sown		
Variety	Thinned		
Type	Sown		
Variety	Thinned		
Type	Sown		
Variety	Thinned		
Type	Sown		
Variety	Thinned		
Type	Sown		
Variety	Thinned		
Type	Sown		
Variety	Thinned		
Type	Sown		
Variety	Thinned		
Type	Sown		
Variety	Thinned		

Cuttings

It is relatively easy to raise new plants by taking cuttings. Pelargoniums, clematis and many shrubs can be raised from softwood or semiripe cuttings taken in spring and summer. Other trees and shrubs can be raised from hardwood cuttings that are taken in autumn. Chrysanthemum cuttings can be taken in the greenhouse in winter.

RIGHT: *Rooted cuttings ready for planting out in position in spring.*

Year .... Year .... Year ....

Plant ....
Taken ....
Planted out ....

Plant ....
Taken ....
Planted out ....

Plant ....
Taken ....
Planted out ....

Plant ....
Taken ....
Planted out ....

Plant ....
Taken ....
Planted out ....

Plant ....
Taken ....
Planted out ....

Plant ....
Taken ....
Planted out ....

Plant ....
Taken ....
Planted out ....

Year .... Year .... Year ....

Plant ....
Taken ....
Planted out ....

Plant ....
Taken ....
Planted out ....

Plant ....
Taken ....
Planted out ....

Plant ....
Taken ....
Planted out ....

Plant ....
Taken ....
Planted out ....

Plant ....
Taken ....
Planted out ....

Plant ....
Taken ....
Planted out ....

Plant ....
Taken ....
Planted out ....

Plant ....
Taken ....
Planted out ....

Plant ....
Taken ....
Planted out ....

Plant ....
Taken ....
Planted out ....

ABOVE: *Hormone rooting powder usually contains a fungicide and so will help prevent rotting, as well as encouraging root growth.*

Weather

It is in a gardener's interest to note the main details of the weather each year. There are two good instruments which can be used. The first is a thermometer. Note the temperature, either each day, or in extremes of heat or cold. For instance, if you know that for 16 consecutive days in the winter the temperature did not rise above freezing-point, it will not surprise you to find that a number of plants have died when spring arrives.

The other useful instrument is a rain gauge. Place this in an open position in the garden with uninterrupted access to the sky. This does need to be checked every morning when it is wet to keep a record of the amount of rain that falls.

RIGHT: *Remember to feed the birds during cold weather, some may be depending on you to help them through the winter.*

	Rainfall	Sunshine	Average Temperature	Comments
January				
February				
March				
April				
May				
June				
July				
August				
September				
October				
November				
December				

	Rainfall	Sunshine	Average Temperature	Comments
January				
February				
March				
April				
May				
June				
July				
August				
September				
October				
November				
December				

Tools and machinery

Lawnmower ....

Supplier ....

Telephone No. ....

Rotivator (Tiller) ....

Supplier ....

Telephone No. ....

Other Machines ....

Supplier ....

Telephone No. ....

Guarantee ....

Serviced ....

Guarantee ....

Serviced ....

Guarantee ....

Serviced ....

Plant suppliers

Name ....

Address ....

....

Telephone No. ....

Name ....

Address ....

....

Telephone No. ....

Name ....

Address ....

....

Telephone No. ....

Name ....

Address ....

....

Telephone No. ....

Name ....

Address ....

....

Telephone No. ....

Name ....

Address ....

....

Telephone No. ....

ABOVE: *Always keeping your equipment well-maintained will help ensure that you will have fewer repair bills.*

ABOVE: *Depending on the size of your garden, you may need a shed. Think carefully about the use of the shed before you buy.*

Index

A

Abelia x grandiflora 191, 204
Abies balsamea 'Nana' 176
Abies cephalonia 'Meyer's Dwarf' 176, *176*
abstract ornaments 115
Acaena microphylla 138
Acanthus spinosus 202, 210, *210*
Acer palmatum atropurpureum 156
Acer platanoides 'Drummondii' 237
Achillea filipendulina 159, 196, 219
    A. filipendulina 'Gold Plate' *159*, 202

Achillea ptarmica 'The Pearl' 162
Achillea tomentosa 138
Actinidia kolomikta 214, *214*
Aethionema grandiflorum 191
afternoon sun plants 191
Agapanthus 158, 196
    A. africanus 236
    A. orientalis 236
Agave americana 21
Ajuga reptans 77, 156, 192, *192*, 236
Akebia quinata 190
Alchemilla mollis 154, 156
alpines 47, 78, 89, 127, 138–9, *302–3*, 361, 421
Alyssum montanum 138
Alyssum saxatile 78, 89, 138, 159, 196, 219, *219*
Amelanchier canadensis 206
Amelanchier laevis 168, *169*
Anagallis 324, *325*
Anchusa azurea 202
Anemone blanda 'White Splendour' 162
Anemone x hybrida 'Honorine Joubert' 162
Angelica archangelica 210, *210*
animal figures 115
animals 18, 218, 219
annuals 7, 18, 143, 197, 209, 214, 219, 236
Antennaria dioica 'Rosea' 138
Anthemis punctata subsp. *cupaniana* 162, *162*
Anthemis tinctoria 159

anthuriums 55
aphids 218, 268
Aponogeton distachyos 131
apples 108, 220, 221, 225, 237
Aquilegia alpina 202
Arabis caucasica 138
Arabis ferdinandi-coburgi 'Variegata' 138
Aralia elata 'Variegata' 170, *170*
arbours 22, 29, *56*, 125, 255
arches 23, *25*, 27, 103, *104–5*, 229, 255
architectural plants 210-11
arctotis 209
Arenaria balearica 138
Argyranthemum (marguerites) 255, 324, 325, 358
Armeria maritima 77, 81, 138, 219
Artemisia absinthium 158
Artemisia arborescens 196, 217
Artemisia ludoviciana 154, 158, *158*
Aruncus dioicus 204, *205*
Arundinaria viridistriata (syn. *Pleioblastus auricomus, P. viridistriatus*) 170, 208
Arundo donax 213
Asarina 107
asparagus 228
aspect 54–5, 190–1
Asplenium scolopendrium 194
Aster alpinus 138
Aster novi-belgii 219
    A. novi-belgii 'Royal Ruby' 160
Astilbe 131, 192
    A. 'Elizabeth Bloom' *204*
    A. x arendsii 204
Astrantia major 192, *192*
aubergines 227
Aubrieta 89, 138, 154
Aucuba japonica 164, 170, 172, 174, 192, 202, 204, 206, 218
    A. japonica 'Variegata' 218
auriculas 246, 333
autumn 66–7, 166–7, 168–9
    plantings 240, 359–67
awnings 124
Azalea 19, 200, 237
Azolla caroliniana 131

B

backyards 21, 39, 50–1
balconies 25, 28, 38, 54–5, 233
bamboo 28
bamboo fencing 93
barbecues 45
barrels 256, 458, 440
basements 39, 50–1
baskets 233, 257, 462
    edible plantings 389
    indoor displays 472
    pink 302
    summer plantings 348
    vibrant colour 312
    white and silver 279, 284, *285*
bathroom plants 469
beans 18, *107*, 220, 229, 388

beds 19, 116, 136, 142–3, 146–7
    feeding and fertilizing 186–7
    maintenance 180
beech 86
bees 218, 458
beetroot 220, 228
Begonia 359, 482
benches 7, 45
Berberis 206, *206*, 218
    B. corallina 201
    B. darwinii 164, 190
    B. thunbergii 159, 168, 174
    B..thunbergii 'Atropurpurea Nana' 86, *218*
    B. wilsoniae 168
    B. x stenophylla 87, 190, 204
Bergenia 81, 164, 174, 192, 236
    B. cordifolia 47, 190
    B. purpurascens 156
berries 7, 240
Betula 19, 167
biennials 219, 236
birds 7, 19, 24, 64, 218, 219
    birdbaths 7, 19, 26, 114, *114*, *148*
black spot 269
bluebells 19
boots 249, 454, *455*
borders 19, 142–3, 145, 146–7, 148–9, 219
    colour schemes 158–63, 166–7
    dwarf conifers *157*, 165, 175, 176–7

    evergreens 164–5
    feeding and fertilizing 186–7
    heathers 178–9
    low-maintenance plants 174–5
    maintenance 180
    planting 150–1
    staking plants 182
    variegated foliage 170–1
botrytis 269
bottle garden 464, *465*
Bougainvillea 21
bowls 461, 476
bricks *43*, 45, 46, 75, 88

bricklaying 90–1
Brunnera macrophylla 192, *193*
bubble fountains 126
Buddleia 11
    B. davidii 172, 196, 206
built-in furniture 120
bulbs 7, 19, 47, 53, 55, 68–9, 89, 143,
    236, 238
butterflies 7, 19, 218, 219, 403, 458
Buxus 22, 87, 142, 213
    B. sempervirens 'Aureovariegata' 170, 192
    B. sempervirens 'Suffruticosa ' 86

C
cacti 21, 54, 461
Calendula officinalis 18
Callicarpa 218

Calluna vulgaris 52, 201, *201*
Caltha palustris 130, 131
Camellia 160, 164, 192, 201
    C. japonica 190, 237
    C. x williamsii 190, 237
cameo gardens 246–7
Campanula 202
    C. carpatica 138
    C. cochleariifolia 138
    C. garganica 138
Campsis radicans 191, *191*
Campsis x tagliabuana
    'Madame Galen' 191
candles 50, 118–19
Canna indica 191
Cardamine pratensis 'Flore Pleno' 204
Carex morrowi 'Evergold' 170
Carex oshimensis 'Evergold' 236
carrots 220, 227, 228
cars 39, 46
Caryopteris x clandonensis 172, 196
    C. x clandonensis 'Heavenly Blue' 202
cascades 128
Casiope 201
Catalpa bignonioides 'Aurea' 210
caterpillars 268

Ceanothus 158, 214, 218
    C. impressus 191
    C. x burkwoodii 158, 164
    C. x deleanus 'Gloire de Versailles' 191
Cedrus deodara 'Golden Horizon' 176
celery 227
Centaurea cyanus 219
Cerastium tomentosum 138
Ceratostigma plumbaginoides 168
Ceratostigma willmottianum 206, 240
Chaenomeles 206
    C. japonica 204-5
    C. x superba 190
chain link fencing 93
Chamaecyparis lawsoniana 'Aurea Densa'
    176, *177*
Chamaecyparis lawsoniana 'Bleu Nantais' 176
Chamaecyparis obtusa 'Nana Gracilis' 176
Chamaemelum nobile (chamomile) 41,
    70, 78
children 22, 448–61
chimney pots 274, 375, 445
Chimonanthus praecox 166, 216
chives 222
choices checklist 15
Choisya ternata 163, 172, 174, 190,
    216, 217
    C. ternata 'Sundance' 159, 164, 236
Chrysanthemum 160, 166, *166*, 209
    C. x superbum (syn. *C. maximum*)
    162, *162*
circles 32–3, 60
    making a miniature pebble circle 79
Cistus 162, 202, *203*, 218
    C. x corbariensis 172
    C. x cyprius 191
    C. x pulverulentus 'Sunset' 191
claire-voyée 100
Clematis 107, 108, 109, 110, 125, *189*,
    214, 445
    C. alpina 109, 190
    C. montana 101, *101*, 190
    C. 'Nelly Moser' 190
    C. 'Prince Charles' 445
    C. tangutica 190
    C. 'The President' *214*
    C. viticella 108
Cleome 209
Clerodendrum trichotomum 168
Clianthus puniceus 208
climbers *18*, 23, 28, 101, 106, 111, 188,
    214–15
    annual 107
    arbours 125
    pillars 110
    shrubs 109
    trees 108
climbing vegetables 228–9
closeboard fencing 92
clover 71
Cobaea scandens 107, 109
cobbles 75
Colchicum 68, 154
    C. speciosum 166
collections 497

colour 29, 55, 143, 242–3, 244–5, 278
    autumn 166–7, 168–9
    black and white 427
    blue and purple 320, *321*, 323, 324, *325*
    blue and silver 158–9
    lime-green and blue 345
    pink 287, *288*, 289, 290, 291–3, 294,
        295, 296, 297, 298, 299, 300, 302
    red 160–1, 310, 311
    variegated 170-1
    vibrant 301, 304, 306, 308, 309, 310,
        311, 312, 313, 314, 315, 316, *317*
    white 162–3, 279, 280, *281*, 282, 283,
        284, *285*, 286
    yellow and gold 159, 310, *311*, 354,
        355, 412, *413*
Colutea arborescens 196, *196*
compost 67, 235, 258
compost areas 14, 22, 30
conifers 47, 49, 179
construction 37, 52
container ponds 126, 128, 456
containers 233, 270, 278
contours 35
Convolvulus cneorum 162, 196
cooking pots 426
copper pots 480, *481*, 482
cordons 224
Cordyline australis 208, *208*, 210
corner sites 41, 253
Cornus 167
    C. alba 52, 168, *168*
    C. alba 'Elegantissima' 170
    C. alba 'Sibirica' 167
    C. canadensis 163, 201

    C. controversa 'Variegata' 210
    C. mas 166
    C. stolonifera 'Flaviramea' 167, 174
Cortaderia selloana 'Aureolinata' 156
Corydalis lutea 138
Cosmos atrosanguineus 247
Cotinus coggyria 52, 174, *174*
Cotoneaster 174, 218

C. *dammeri* 81, 165
C. *frigidus* 206
C. *horizontalis* 168, *174*, 190
C. 'Hybridus Pendulus' 237
cottage gardens 18, 47, 228, 346
Cotula coronopifolia 71
Cotula squalida 77
courgettes 227, 229
courtyard gardens 17, 25, *25*
Crambe cordifolia 205, 211
crazy paving 77
crevice plants 77
Crinodendron hookerianum 190
Crocosmia 191
C. 'Lucifer' 160, *161*
Crocus 47, 68, 154, 238
C. *speciosus* 166
C. *tommasinianus* 166, *166*
cucumbers 227, 229
curved borders 146
cuttings 266
Cyclamen coum 166
Cyclamen hederifolium (syn.
C. *neapolitanum*) 166
Cynara cardunculus 181
Cytisus battandieri 216
Cytisus multiflorus (syn. C. *albus*) 162
Cytisus x kewensis 172

D
Daboecia cantabrica 200, 201
Dahlia 160
Daphne bholua 'Jacqueline Postill' 252
Daphne mezereum 216, *216*, 218
Daphne odorata 'Aureomarginata' 247
Datura (syn. Brugmansia) 21, 211, *211*, 483
decking 54, 59, 80
deep beds 226
Delphinium 158, *158*, 202
designing plans 32–7, 150–1
Deutzia scabra 190
D. *scabra* 'Plena' 191, 202
diagonals 32–3, 60–1
Dianthus 78, *160*, 191, 202–3
D. *barbatus* 'Scarlet Beauty' *203*

D. *deltoides* 138, *138*
Dicentra 236
D. *spectabilis* 192
Digitalis 190
D. *grandiflora* (syn. D. *orientalis*) 205
Dipsacus 219
diseases 235, 268–9
ditches 100
Dodecathon meadia 190
drawing plans 34–5, 36–7
drives 39, 46, 47, 48, 49
dry stone walling 89, *89*
Dryas octopetala 138, 191
dustbins 30
dwarf conifers 89, *157*, 165, 175, 176–7

E
eating outdoors 6, 24, 42, 124–5, 250–1
Eccremocarpus scaber 107, 109, 110, 191
Echinacea purpurea 191
Echinops ritro 191, 196
edges 47, 59, 60–1, 77, 147
Eichhornia crassipes 130
Elaeagnus pungens 206
E. *pungens* 'Maculata' *164*, 165, 170, 174
E. x *ebbingei* 206
E. x *ebbingei* 'Gilt Edge' *206*
E. x *ebbingei* 'Limelight' 170
electrical installations 117
Elodea canadensis 131, 134
entrances 252, *254*
Epimedium grandiflorum 201
Epimedium perralderianum 156, 192
Eranthis hyemalis 68
erecting fences 94–5
Erica 165, 166, 201
E. *carnea* 52, *164*, 173, 174
E. *gracilis* 240
E. *hyemalis* 240
Erigeron 219
Erinus alpinus 138
Eryngium agavifolium 236
Eryngium variifolium 197
Erysimum cheiri (syn. *Cheiranthus barbatus*) 203, 329
Escallonia 84, *160*, 218
E. *macrantha* 65
espaliers 50, 101, 221, 224
eucalyptus 11, 217
Eucryphia glutinosa 162
Euonymus fortunei 52, 81, 165, 170, 190, 214
E. *fortunei* 'Emerald Gaiety' *108*
E. *fortunei* 'Emerald 'n' Gold' *52*, 156
Euphorbia 27
E. *griffithii* 190
evergreens 7, 46, 55, 81, 164–5, 236, 366, 367, 370, 376, 377, 420
exotic style 21, 51, 55, 189, 208–9

F
fans 221, 224
Fatsia japonica (syn. *Aralia sieboldii*) 156, 157, 175, 208, 211

feeding 186–7
container plants 235, 259
feet on containers 261
fences 7, 84, 92–3, 94–5, 101
fennel 222
ferns 19, *50*, 51, *408*, 411
borders 194–5
fertilizers 186–7, 258, 259
Festuca glauca 154–5, 156, 158

flooring 54, 78–9
flowers with vegetables 228–9
focal points 7, 19, 20, 26-7, 51, 102–3, 189
foliage 7, 55, 215, 348, 408, 432, 433, 434, *435*
borders 156–7
scented 217
formal style 16–17, 86, 142
Forsythia 87
F. *suspensa* 190
F. x *intermedia* 159, 207
Fothergilla major 169, 201
fountains 126, 128, 436
Fremontodendron 'California Glory' 191
Fritillaria 68
F. *imperialis* 69, 191
front gardens 39, 46–7, 48–9, 85
frost 54, 236, 240
fruit 7, 221, 224–5, 228, 378, 386, 389, 392
fruit trees 101, 221, 224
Fuchsia 160, 236, 252, 284, *285*, 298, 299, 359, 436, 442, *443*, 459, 480, *481*
F. *magellanica* 'Versicolor' 170, 173
furniture 21, 57, 103, 120–1, 122–3

G
Galanthus 238
G. *nivalis* 47, 69, 155, 190
garden flares 118, *118*
garden layouts 28, 32–3, 42, 46–7, 48–9, 60–1, 144
Garrya elliptica 190, 207, 215, *215*
gates 27, 85

Genista tinctoria 172, 173, 197
Gentiana acaulis 138
Gentiana septemfida 138
Gentiana sino-ornata 138, 201
Geranium 407
    G. cinereum 'Ballerina' 191
    G. 'Johnson's Blue' 191
    G. subcaulescens 'Splendens' 138
    G. x oxonianum 108
gerberas 209
gilded pots 119
Gladiolus 160–1
globe artichokes 220

gnomes 115
grass borders 156–7
grass substitutes 70–1
gravel 20, 41, 46, 47, 49, 58, 82–3
Griselinia littoralis 175, 212, 213
ground cover 11, 58, 59, 81, 152
growing bags 221, 222, 227
Gunnera manicata 208, 211
Gypsophila 203
    G. paniculata 155, 162
    G. repens 138

H
ha-has 100
Hakonechloa macra 'Alboaurea' 156, *157*
Halimiocistus sahucii 162
Hamamelis mollis 166, 190, 216
hanging baskets 227, 257, 262–3, 264, 408
    autumn plantings 359, 364
    blue and purple 318–19, 322, 326–7
    children's 452
    edible plantings 385, 388, 390,
        391, 392
    inspirational plantings 432
    pink 291–2, 294, 295, 297, 298,
        299, 300
    scented 396, *397*, 400, *401*
    shade 409, 410, 411, 412, *413*
    spring plantings 338, *339*
    summer plantings 341, 342, *343*, 346,
        347, 354, *355*, 357–8
    sun 415
    vibrant colour 309, 310, *311*, 314

winter plantings 374
hard landscaping 7, 11, *15*, 18, *59*
heathers 87, 178–9
Hebe 47, 165, 175, 197, 218, 237, *243*
    H. 'Midsummer Beauty' 173
    H. x franciscana 'Variegata' *165*, 170
Hedera helix (ivy) 55, 101, 109, *188*,
    125, 190, *207*, 215, 218, 375, 418,
    428, *429*
Hedera colchica 190
hedges 7, 16, 23, 28, 46, 86–7, 84, 219
height *38*, 102, 104, 106–7, 110–11,
    112–13, 237
Helenium 'Bruno' 161, *161*
Helenium 'Waldtraut' 191
Helianthemum 'Fire Dragon' *138*, 161
    H. nummularium *196*, 198, 203
Helianthus annuus (sunflower) 219, 360
Helichrysum italicum 191
Heliotropium 247
Helleborus 27, 192
    H. foetidus 190
    H. niger 167
    H. orientalis 167, *167*
Hemerocallis 131, 159, *159*, 161, 175
    H. 'Burning Daylight' 205
herbs 7, *10*, 17, 24, 87, 121, 217, 221,
    222–3, 228, 247, 378, 379–81,
    385–8, 390
    herb wheel, making 223
Hesperis matronalis 219
Heuchera 'Pewter Moon' 156-7
Hibiscus syriacus 175
    H. syriacus 'Blue Bird' 158
Hippophaë rhamnoides 52
hit-and-miss fencing 92
hoops 112-13
Hordeum jubatum 155
Hosta 58, 131, 157, 171, 191, 193, 248
    H. fortunei albopicta 170
    H. fortunei var. *hyacinthina* 156
houseplants 55, 209
Houttynia cordata 130, 171, *171*
    H. cordata 'Chameleon' 171
hoverflies 218
human figures 115
Humulus lupulus 108, 110, 125
    H. lupulus 'Aureus' 101, 191, 205, 215
Hydrangea 148
    H. macrophylla 52
    H. paniculata 'Grandiflora' 52
    H. petiolaris 108, 190, 215
Hypericum 218
    H. calycinum *159*, *172*, 173, 193
    H. 'Hidcote' 159, 190
    H. olympicum 138, 139
    H. x moserianum 'Tricolor' 171
hyssop 223

I
Iberis sempervirens 'Snowflake' 139
Ilex (holly) *149*, 165, 169, 171, 175, 190,
    213, 218
    I. aquifolium 207
    I. aquifolium 'Aurea Marginata' *165*

    I. x altaclarensis 'Lawsoniana' *207*
Impatiens (busy Lizzies) 236, 409
Imperata cylindrica 'Rubra' 191
indoor gardens 463, 470–1, 476
indoor topiary 473
informal style 18–19, 86, 287
insects 18, 24, 218, 219
interlap fencing 92
Ipomoea 107, 109
    I. tricolor 'Heavenly Blue' 208, 209
Iris 127
    I. laevigata 130
    I. pallida 'Variegata' 171, *171*
    I. pseudacorus 131
    I. pseudacorus 'Variegatus' 171
    I. reticulata 238
    I. sibirica 131
    I. unguicularis 167, *167*
iron furniture 120
island beds 136, 144

J
Japanese style 20, *20*, 28, 32, 440
Jasminum 24, 109
    J. nudiflorum 167, 190, 215, *215*
    J. officinale 215, 216, 247
Jerusalem artichokes 212
Juncus effusus 'Spiralis' 130
Juniperus communis 'Compressa' 176
Juniperus horizontalis 176
Juniperus scopulorum/virginiana
    'Skyrocket' 211
Juniperus virginiana 'Sulphur Spray' (syn.
    J. chinensis 'Sulphur Spray') 176

K
Kalmia latifolia 201
Kerria japonica 'Pleniflora' 190
kitchen gardens 220–1

Kniphofia 175, *175*, 197, 208, 211
knot gardens 16–17
Kolkwitzia amabilis 191, 203

L
L-shaped gardens 41
Lablab purpureus (syn. *Dolichos lablab*) 107

labour-saving tips 15, 35
Laburnum 237
ladybirds 218
Lagenaria 107
lanterns 50, 118, *118*
Lathyrus grandiflorus 205
Lathyrus odoratus (sweet peas) 107, 109,

236, 342
Laurus nobilis (bay) 217, 222, 252
Lavandula 24, 47, 78, 87, 173, 197, 216,
   218, *394*, 400, *401*
   L. angustifolia 155
   L. angustifolia 'Hidcote' 191
   L. stoechas 191
Lavatera olbia 52
lawns 15, 26, 58, 60–1, 64–5, 66–7,
   68–9, 69–70
   laying turf 63
   sowing grass seed 62
laying bricks and blocks 91
laying gravel beds 83
laying paving 73, 77
lead chimney 274
legal restrictions 39, 80, 84–5
Lemna 131, 133
lemon balm 217, 222
lettuces 220, 227, 228, 247
Leucanthemum x superbum (syn.
   Chrysanthemum maximum) 205
Leucojum aestivum 162
levels *15*, 40, 42–3, 61
Leycesteria formosa 173, *173*, 207, 218
lighting 7, 50, 103, 116–17
Ligustrum 171, 218
   L. ovalifolium 86, 207
   L. ovalifolium 'Aureum' 159, 212,
      213, *213*
Lilium 161, 162–3, 191, 208, *209*, 441
   L. regale 236, 247
Limnanthes douglasii 18, 219
Liriope muscari 175, 193
lily-of-the-valley 238
Lobelia 89, 236, 278
   L. cardinalis 161

long gardens 17, 19, 27, 39, 40
Lonicera (honeysuckle) 24, 108, 109,
   110, 125
   L. nitida 86, *86*
   L. nitida 'Baggesen's Gold' 159, 165,
      193, 212, 213
   L. periclymenum 190, 215, 216, 218
   L. pileata 52
   L. x brownii (syn. *L. sempervirens*)
      'Dropmore Scarlet' 203
   L. x japonica 212, 215
low-maintenance gardens 11, 20, 46, 174–5
Lunaria annua 219
Lupinus arboreus 173
Lychnis chalcedonica 161, *161*
M
Mahonia 218
   M. aquifolium 52, 193
   M. 'Charity' 165, 167, 173, 211, *211*,
      216, 240
   M. japonica 175, 190
mail order plants 267
maintenance
   beds and borders 180
   container plants 235, 259, 260
   low-maintenance gardens 11, 20,
      46, 174–5
   ponds 132–3
Malus (apples) 108, 220, 221, 225, 237
   M. 'John Downie' 169
   M. tschonoskii 169
marjoram 222
Matteucia struthiopteris 157, *194*
Matthiola bicornis 51, 216
Matthiola incana 216, *216*
mealy bugs 268
measuring garden site 34–5
mechanical aids 66
Meconopsis betonicifolia 201
Mediterranean style 7, 21, *21*, 89, 208–9,
   314, 438, *439*
Mentha (mint) 222, 229
Mexican painted pots *25*, 272
Mimulus 131
Mina lobata (syn. *Ipomoea lobata*) 107
mirrors 29
Miscanthus sacchariflorus 213
Miscanthus sinensis 'Silberfeder' 157
Molucella laevis 191
Monarda 'Cambridge Sacrlet' 161
morning sun plants 190
mulching 179, 183, 184–5, 265
Myriophyllum 131, 134

N
Narcissi 55, 68, 69, *250*, 329
narrow gardens *17*, 19, 27, 39, 40
natural predators on pests 269
neighbours 84–5, 116
Nepeta 219
   N. x faassenii 155, 158, 197
Nerine bowdenii 167, *167*
Nicotiana 51, *51*, 55
novelty containers 51, 233, 257
   boots *249*, 454, *455*

chimney pots 274, 375, 445
cooking pot 426
indoor plantings 479
tin bath 444
tyres 453
watering-can planter 449
wine case 381

O
oleanders 21
Olearia x haastii 52, 163, *163*, 207
onions 227
optical illusions 29
orchid basket 498
ornamental vegetables *226*, *242*, *251*
ornaments 19, 21, 103, 114–15, 116
Orontium aquaticum 131
Osmanthus x burkwoodii (syn. *x Osmarea
   burkwoodii*) 207
Osteospermum 191, 197, 208, 236, 308
   O. jacundum 196
   O. 'Whirligig' 163
oval beds 146
overwintering container plants 260
Oxalis adenophylla 139

P
Pachysandra terminalis 52, 81, *171*, 193
   P. terminalis 'Variegata' 171
palms 21, 466
panel fencing 92, 94
Papaver orientale 161, 191

parsley 388
parterres 16-17
Parthenocissus 190
   P. henryana 190
passageways 39
Passiflora 109
paths 7, 15, 58, 64, 76–7
patios 28, 38, 42-3, 44–5
Paulownia tomentosa 211
paving 7, 15, 18, 21, *42*, 43, 54, 58, 72–3,
   74–5, 76–7, 78–9

paved gardens 17
peas 220, 228
peat beds 136
pebbles 76, 78–9
pedestals 115
Pelargonium 21, 161, 236, 246, 249, 291, 297, 402
Pennisetum villosum (syn. *P. longistylum*) 157
Penstemon 191
peppers 227
perennials 7, 18, 89, 143, 236
pergolas 23, 44–5, 103, 104–5, 188, 229
Pernettya (gaultheria) 175, 218, 240
   P. mucronata 52, 169, *169*, 201
Perovskia atriplicifolia 158, 197
Persicaria bistorta 'Superba' (syn. *Polygonum bistorta*) 205

pests 235, 268–9
Petunia 236, 255, *278*, 428, *429*
Phalaris arundinacea 'Picta' *163*
Philadelphus 52, *52*, 163, 207, 217
   P. coronarius 'Aureus' 86, 159, 173
Phlomis fruticosa 197, *197*, 202, 203
Phlox douglasii 138, 139
Phlox paniculata 205
   P. paniculata 'White Admiral' *163*
Phlox subulata 139
Phormium 21, 41, 101, 165, 171, 197, 205, 208, 211
   P. 'Dazzler' 161
   P. tenax 205
Picea abies 'Gregoryana' 176, *177*
Picea glauca 'Echiniformis' 177
   Picea g. var. *albertiana* 'Alberta Globe' 177
   *Picea g.*var. *albertiana* 'Conica' 177
Picea pungens 'Globosa' 177
Picea pungens 'Montgomery' 177
picket fencing 93
pillars 110–11
pimpernels 324
Pinus mugo 'Corley's Mat' 177
Piptanthus laburnifolius 190
pithoi 27
planning designs 32–7, 150–1

plant size 7, 11, 151
plant supports 261
planting:
   conifer and heather mixed bed 179
   containers 261
   fern border 195
   ground cover 152
   herbaceous plants 151
   hedge 87
   ponds130–1
   rock garden 138–9
   shrubs 153
   waterlilies 130
plastic containers 261, 301, 324, 325, 344–5, 350, 366, *367*, 382, *383*
plastic fencing 93
plastic furniture 120
play areas 22
Pleioblastus auricomus (syn. *P. viridistriatus*) 157
plinths 115
pointed gardens 40
pollution-tolerant plants 206–7
Polyanthus 238
Polygonum baldschuanica (syn. *Fallopia baldschuanica*) 108, 125, 213, *213*, 215
ponds 19, 126, 128–9, 132–3, 134–5, 136
   miniature 425, 456
   planting 130–1
Pontederia cordata 130
Portulaca 209
post and chain fencing 93
potagers 226, 227
potatoes 221, 227
Potentilla 87, 218
   P. atrosanguinea 161
   P. fruticosa 159, 173, 175, *202*, 203
   P. tabernaemontani 138
pots 256, 264
   autumn plantings 360
   children's plantings 459–60
   inspirational plantings 427, 438, *439*, 442, *443*, 445–6
   scented plantings 247, 336, 399, 407
   shade 414
   spring plantings 330, *331*, 333, 337
   summer plantings 356
   winter plantings 368, 370, 376
potting-on 267
powdery mildew 269
power tools 66
primroses 19
Primula 23, 131, 238, 246
privacy 7, 23, 52–3, 84, 88, 96, 246
propagating plants 266–7
pruning 11
Prunus 'Amanogawa' 237
Prunus subhirtella 'Pendula' (syn. *P.* 'Autumnalis Pendula')167
Pulsatilla vulgaris 139
pumps 134–5
Pyracantha 190, 215, *215*, 218
   P. 'Orange Glow' 169
Pyrus salicifolia 'Pendula' 237

R
radishes 227, 228
raised beds 45, 136
ramblers 96
ranch-style fencing 93, 95
Raoulia ayustralis 138, 139
rectangles 32–3, 60
red spider mite 268
refuse areas 7, 14
Reseda odorata 191
Rhamnus frangula 218
Rheum palmatum (rhubarb) 208, *209*, 225, 228
Rhodochiton atrosanguineum 107
rhododendrons 19, 237
Rhodohypoxis baurii 138, 201
Rhus typhina (syn. *R. hirta*) 169
Ribes sanguineum 175, 218
rock gardens 19, 49, 126–7, 218
Rodgersia pinnata 'Superba' *204*, 205
romance 35
Romneya coulteri 197
roof gardens 25, 28, 38, 39, 52–3, 233
Rosa 17, 24, 47, *86*, 87, 108, 110, 129, 142, 154-5, 161, *188*, 215, 216
   R. 'American Pillar' *110*, *111*
   R. 'Bourbon Queen' 155
   R. 'Cardinal Richelieu' 155
   R. 'Constance Spry' 155
   R. 'Dublin Bay' *98*
   R. 'Kew Rambler' *110*
   R. rugosa 155, 190
Rosmarinus officinalis 87, 165, *165*, 191,

191, 197, 217, 222, 223, 229, 396
Rubus cockburnianus 'Golden Vale' 157
Ruscus aculeatus 193
rushes 127
rust 269
rustic poles, joining 105

S
safety considerations 52, 117, 118
Salix alba Chermesina 167
Salix caprea pendula 237
Salix helvetica 109, *109*

Salix matsudana 'Tortuosa' 211, *211*
salpiglossis 209
Salvia discolor 247
Salvia officinalis 217, 229
   S. officinalis 'Icterina' 171
   S. officinalis 'Purpurascens' 157
   S. officinalis 'Tricolor' 191
Salvia sclarea 181
Salvinia braziliensis 130
sandpits 22
Santolina chamaecyparissus 159, 165, 197
Sarcococca hookeriana humilis 193, *193*, 217
saucers 261
Saxifraga 139
   S. x umbrosa 193
Scabiosa 'Butterfly Blue' 203
Scabiosa causica 219
scale drawings 35, 150
scent 7, 24, 51, 70, 124, 188, 116–17, 233, 468
   foliage 217
   hanging baskets 396, *397*, 400, *401*
   pots 247, 336, 399, 407
   windowboxes 395, 397, 402–3, 406
Scilla 238
Scirpus 'Zebrina' 130
screening 7, 14, 23, 25, 28–9, 53, 55, 88–9, 98, 255
   plants 212–23
sculptural plants 210–11
sculptures 115
seaside garden style *246*, 450, *451*
seating areas 22, 23
seats 19, 41, 45, *102*, *122*, *123*
   tree seats 41, 121

Sedum 138
   S. 'Autumn Joy' *219*
   S. lydium 138
   S. spathulifolium 'Cape Blanco' 139
   S. spectabile 197, *197*, 219
   S. spurium 139
seed sowing 62, 266
Sempervivum 138, 191
   S. ballsii 139

Senecio 'Sunshine' 86, 159, 165, 173, 191
setts 75
shade 7, 11, 51, 188, 189, 408–14
   plants 190, 192–3
shapes 28, 32–3, 42, 46–7, 48–9, 60–1, 144
shared gardens 100
sheds 7, *13,14*, 22, 30
shelter 7, 23
shelving 31
shrubs 11, 14, 28, 40, 42, 45, 100, 108–9, 142–3, 153, 218, 237
   quick growing 172–3
sink gardens 136
   autumn plantings 361
Skimmia 218
   S. japonica 169, *169*, 193, 217
slopes 35, 43, 38
snails 133, 268
soft landscaping 141
soil 198–9
   acid 200–1
   alkaline (chalk) 202–3
   clay 204–5
   soil mixes 235, 258
Solanum bapsicastrum 240
Solanum jasminoides 110
Soleirolia soleirolia 58
Solidago 159, 219, *219*
Sorbus 169, *169*
sound 24, 50, 124
spinach 227, 228
Spiraea 'Arguta' 163
Spiraea japonica 52
Spiraea x bumalda 173, *173*
Spirogyra 133
spring plantings 238, 329–39
square gardens 41
Stachys lanata (syn. *S. byzantina*) 47, 157, 159, 197
staking border plants 182
star-jasmine 404
statues 26, *29*, *103*, *115*
stems, colourful 167
Stephanotis floribunda 109
stepping stones 48, 49, 59
steps 42–3, 51, 254
Sternbergia lutea 167
stone gardens 20, 32
stop-overs 224
storage 30–1
Stratiotes aloides 131
strawberries 225, 251, 305, 389, 392
streams 19
strelitzias 55
succulents 54, 247
summer plantings 238, 340–58
sun plants 191, 196–7, 408
sundials 26, *103*, 114
Symphoricarpos 218
   S. albus 193, *193*
Syringa 218
   S. vulgaris 203, *203*, 207, 217, *217*
   S. vulgaris 'Madame Lemoine" 163

T
table decorations 250-1
Tamarix tetranda 52, 207
Taxus baccata (yew) 86
   T. baccata 'Repandens' 177
   T. baccata 'Standishii' 177
temporary supports for climbers 106–7
terracotta containers 256, 260, 330, *331*, 333, 368, 370, 436, 446, *447*
   pots 21, 31, 223, 260, *270*, 368, 370, 386, *387*, 399, 414, 427, 438, *439*
   windowboxes 282, 293, 304, 306, *307*, 316, 332, 353, 379, 384, 398, 402, 417
terrarium 474, *475*
testing soil 199
Thuja 23

   T. occidentalis 'Ericoides' 177
   T. orientalis 'Aurea Nana' (syn. *Platycladus orientalis* 'Aurescens') 177
   T. orientalis 'Rosedalis' (syn. *Platycladus orientalis* 'Rosedalis') 177
   T. orientalis 'Sieboldii' *177*
Thunbergia alata 107
Thymus 218, 222, 229, 247
   T. serpyllum 70, 77, 78, 139
Tiarella cordifolia 193
tiles 21, 54, 75, 78, *78*, 79
Tillaea recurva 131
tin containers 257, 320, *321*
   bath 444
   spring plantings 336
   tin can plant nursery 271
tomatoes 221, 227, *227*, 386, 390, 393
topiary 237, *241*, 368, 428, 446, *447*
   indoor topiary 473
touch 24, 124, 247
town gardens 28–9
Trachelospermum jasminoides 404
Trachycarpus fortunei 21
Tradescantia x andersoniana 205
trees 11, 14, 28–9, 40, 45,47, 108–9,

167, 237
    fruit trees 101, 221, 224
    tree seats 41, 121
trellis 23, 28–9, 28, 30, 50, 96–7, 98–9, 212
triangulation 35
Trifolium repens 71
Trillium grandiflorum 201
tripods 27, 112–13
Tropaeolum (nasturtiums) 89, 110, 236
    T. majus 107, 109
    T. peregrinum (syn. *T. canariense*) 107, 109
    T. speciosus 190
tropical plants 208–9
troughs 56, 138, 256, 361
    inspirational plantings 421
trugs 418
    inspirational plantings 422, *423*
    winter plantings 369
tubs 14, 236
    spring plantings 329, 334, *335*
    trees and shrubs 237
    vegetables 227, 247
Tulipa 68, 161, 244
turf laying 63
turnips 227
tyres 453

U
Ulex 218
    U. europaeus 175, 197
umbrellas 124
urns 7, *25*, *27*, 252, *253*, *260*
    inspirational plantings 441
utilities 7, 14, 28, 30–1

V
variegated plants 170–1
vegetables 7, 220–1, 226–7, 378, 382, *383*, 386, 388, 390, 393, 467
    ornamental 226, *242*, *251*
    tubs 227, 247
    windowboxes 457
    with flowers 228–9
verandas 54–5

Verbascum 203
Verbena 217, 236, 246, *251*, 319, 406
verdigris bucket 273
Veronica prostrata 139
verticals 38, 102, 104, 106–7, 110–11, 112–13, 237
Viburnum 218
    V. davidii 175, 193
    V. plicatum 163
    V. tinus 86, 165, 167, 175, 237, 240
    V. x bodnatense 217
    V. x bodnatense 'Dawn' 167
villandry planter 404, *405*
Vinca major 190
Vinca minor 'Variegata' 171, *171*, 193
vine weevils 268
Viola 78, *235*, *243*, 246, 262, 308, 313, 319, 369
    V. x wittrockiana 155
viruses 269
Vitis coignetiae 44, 108, 191, 215

W
wall baskets 51
    pink 287, 290, 296
    silver and white 286
    summer plantings 340, 352
    vibrant colour 313, 315
    winter plantings 377
wall features 115, 128
wall fountains 436
wall pots 433
wall shrubs 50, 214–15
wall spouts 126
wallflowers 329
walls 7, 21, 23, 42, 84–5, 88–9, 98–9, 101, 138, 212, 254
washing lines 14
wasps 218
water features 19, *24*, 49, 50, 116, 126–7
water plants 127
water snails 133
watering 53, 235, 264-5
watering-can planter 449
waterlilies 127, 130
    'Froebelli' 131
    'James Brydon' 131
    Laydekeri lilacea 131
    Pygmeae helvola 131
    'Rose Arey' 131
water lily basket 425
weeds 59, 64–5, 81, 183, 228
    pond weeds 133
weevils 218
Weigela 173, *173*, 218
    W. florida 207
    W. florida 'Variegata' 171
white-flowered plants 51, 189
whitefly 269
wicker baskets 261
    inspirational plantings 430, *431*
wildlife 7, 189, 218–19
wildlife gardens 18–19
wind 38, 55, 408

wind chimes 50
wind-tolerant plants 52
windbreak screens 53
windowboxes 51, 55, 220–1, 222, 225, 227, 256–7, 264
    autumn plantings 362, 363, 365–6
    blue and purple 320, *321*, 323, 324, *325*
    edible plantings 379–80, 382, *383*, 384, 393
    inspirational plantings 419–20, 424, 428, 429, 434, *435*, 437
    pink 288, 289, 293
    scented plantings 395, 397, 402–3, 406
    shell 275
    spring plantings 332
    summer plantings 344–5, 349–*51*, 353

    sun 416–17
    vegetables 457
    vibrant colour 301, 304, 306, 308, 316, *317*
    white and silver 280, *281*, 282, *283*
    winter plantings 371, 372, *373*
wine case 381
winter 134–5
    plantings 240, 368–77
Wisteria 215, 217, *217*
wood anemones 19
wooden furniture 120
woodland gardens 19, 337

X
x Cupressocyparis leylandii 86

Y
Yucca 21, *21*, 41, *101*, 175, 197, 209, 211
    Y. filamentosa 'Variegata' 165, 237
    Y. gloriosa 'Variegata' 165

Z
Zantedeschia aethiopica 209, *209*

Acknowledgements

The publishers would like to thank all those who provided locations, materials and equipment for the special photography in this book. Specially commissioned photographs were provided by the following:

Peter Anderson: 62, 63, 66, 67, 68, 132, 133, 134, 135, 154bl, 155tr, 156t, 156b, 157tr, 176, 177, 178, 182 top row, 182br, 183, 192, 193, 200r, 201r and 204br.

Sue Atkinson: 157tl, 157b, 160tr, 161tl, 162l, 163br, 196, 202l, 202r, 204, 205t, 205b, 206l, 229tr,

Jonathan Buckley: 27bl, 52l, 52r, 96c, 96r, 97, 98, 99, 106, 107, 108, 109, 110, 111, 112, 113, 163t, 163bl, 180, 197, 186, 190b, 191, 200l, 203, 206, 207bl, 207tr, 207br, 229tl, 229c and 229b.

John Freeman: 14, 16b, 17t, 19t, 20, 31br, 35, 38t, 39, 44b, 45t, 45b, 50b, 51b, 53b, 57, 58t, 59t, 61, 64t, 64b, 65tl, 65tr, 65bl, 69, 71, 73, 74, 75, 77, 81, 82, 83 top row, 83cl, 83bl, 84, 86t, 87 top row, 87c, 87bc, 87br, 89t, 90t, 91, 92tl, 92tr, 94, 95tl, 95 steps, 102, 103b, 104, 105 steps, 114, 115, 120, 127br, 128, 129, 130, 131tr, 136b, 137, 139 steps, 142, 145b, 146, 147, 148, 149b, 151, 152 steps, 153, 179, 182bl, 184, 185, 187, 188tr, 188br, 189b, 192, 193, 197, 220tr, 220br, 223, 227b, 236m, 236b, 237b, 238m, 240, 246, 254tl, 255br, 258, 260r, 261mr, 265r, 266, 267, 284, 298, 299, 329, 330, 331, 333, 334, 335, 336, 337, 348, 356, 360, 361, 364, 365, 368, 369, 370, 371, 372, 373, 375, 376, 381, 386, 387, 389, 395, 404, 405, 425, 426, 427, 433, 436, 438, 439, 440, 441, 442, 443, 444, 445, 449, 453, 454, 455, 456, 457, 458, 459, 460, 461, 466, 467, 469, 470, 471, 477, 478, 479, 480, 481, 482 and 483.

Don Last: 269r, 463, 464, 465, 472, 473, 474, 475, 476 and 477.

Marie O'Hara: 23l, 31t, 132 and 204br.

Debbie Patterson: 22, 23c, 23tr, 23b, 24l, 24r, 25tl, 25tr, 25b, 26, 27tl, 27tr, 27br, 28t, 28b, 29tl, 29tr, 29b, 30t, 30b, 31l, 78t, 78b, 79, 96l, 118b, 118t, 119, 122l, 122r, 123, 124, 125, 155b, 236t, 237t, 238t, 241, 242t, 244t, 244m, 245, 247, 250, 251, 255, 260l, 270, 271, 272, 273, 274 and 285.

The publishers would also like to thank the following picture libraries from allowing their photographs to be reproduced for this book:

Derek Fell: 19b, 53t, 55t, 55b, 95tr, 141, 221 and 226t.

The Garden Picture Library: 16t (Marijke Heuff), 54 (Ron Sutherland), 80 (John Duane), 116 (Jane Legate), 222t (Lynne Brotchie) and 222b (J S Sira).

Robert Harding: 42b.

The Harpur Garden Library: 10 (designed by Maggie Geiger, NYC), 15t (a garden in Canterbury), 15b (designed by Michael Balston), 17b (designed by Trevor Frankland), 21t (designed by John Patrick, VIC), 38b (designed by Anthony Noel, London), 42t (designed by Berry's Garden co., Golders Green), 43b (designed by Christopher Masson, London), 44t (designed by Malcolm Hillier, London), 56 (designed by Christpher Masson, London), 58b (designed by Wayne Winterrowd & Joe Eck, London), 59b

(designed by Anne Alexander-Sinclair), 60t (designed by Ernie Taylor, Great Barr), 60b (a garden in Tayside), 72t (designed by Berry's Garden Co., Golders Green), 76 (designed by Hilary McMahon for Costin's Nursery, RHS Chelsea), 85b (designed by Anthony Noel, London), 85t (Fudlers Hall, Mashbury), 88t (designed by Jan Martinez, Kent), 93b (designed by Bruce Kelly, NYC), 105br (designed by Arabella Lennox-Boyd, 126b (designed by Simon Fraser, London), 136t (Joe Elliot, Broadwell, Gloucs), 140 (designed by Beth Chatto), 141 (designed by Ernie Taylor, Great Barr), 144 (Bank House, Borwich) and 149t (Home Farm, Balscotte, Oxon).

Peter McHoy: 16b, 50t, 51t, 65br, 70t, 70b, 72, 77bl, 83br, 86b, 87bl, 88b, 89b, 92b, 93t, 100, 101t, 101b, 117, 131b, 137b, 138t, 138bl, 138br, 139t, 155tl, 158t, 158c, 158b, 159t, 159c, 159b, 161tr, 161b, 162r,

164t, 164b, 165t, 165c, 165b, 166t, 166b, 167t, 167c, 167b, 168t, 168b, 169t, 169bl, 169br, 170t, 170b, 171tl, 171tr, 171bl, 171br, 172t, 172b, 173tl, 173tr, 173b, 174t, 174b, 175, 192tc192b, 193t, 193m, 193b, 196l, 196r, 197t, 197b, 203tl, 203bl, 208t, 208b, 209tr, 209br, 209l, 210t, 210b, 211tl, 211tr, 211b, 212l. 212r, 213t, 213b, 214t, 214b, 215t, 215bl, 215br, 216t, 216b, 217t, 217b, 218, 219t, 219c, 219b, 220bl, 224r, 225r, 226b, 227t, 239, 244, 249, 252r, 268 and 269l.

Jacqui Hurst: 18, 103t, 126t, 127t, 127bl, 143t, 143b, 145t, 152tl, 188l, 189t and 228.

Lucy Mason: 131tl.

All container projects were created by Stephanie Donaldson and photographed by Marie O'Hara unless otherwise stated.
Project contributors:

Clare Bradley: 449, 453, 454, 455, 456, 457, 458, 460, 461, 464 and 465.

Blaise Cook: 246, 252l, 255br, 266, 267, 284, 298, 299, 433, 436, 442, 443, 459, 480 and 481.

Tessa Eveleigh: 236, 238t, 241, 242t, 244t, 244m, 245, 247, 248, 250, 251 and 255t.

Peter McHoy: 244, 249, 252r, 461, 463, 464, 465, 472, 473, 474, 475, 476 and 477.

Lesley Harle: 270.

Karin Hossack: 25, 271 and 272

Cleo Mussi: 79.

Liz Wagstaff: 119, 273 and 27.

t=top, b=bottom, m=middle, l=left, r=right